THE BLUE THUMB GUIDE

THE BLUE THUMB GUIDE

TO WORKING ON YOUR HOUSE

BY BILL SCHULTZ

Prism Editions
Chronicle Books
San Francisco

Book design by Robert Harriman.

Library of Congress Cataloging in Publication Data

Schultz, Bill.
   The blue thumb guide to working on your
house.

   A Prism edition.
   Includes index.
   1. Dwellings—Remodeling.   I. Title.
TH4816.S287   643'.7   78-1992
ISBN 0-87701-111-7

Chronicle Books
870 Market Street
San Francisco, CA 94102
A Prism Edition

CONTENTS

ABOUT THIS BOOK

The material for this book was gathered over several years of projects and many conversations with friends who had bought old houses—as I had—and fixed them up out of the grocery money. The procedures aren't always orthodox, but they do work—and they don't require shop tools or advanced skills.

All of the projects outlined here can be completed with handtools, including three that use electricity: a circular saw (about $40), a ⅜-inch electric hand drill (about $40) and a saber saw ($15-$30). You'll need the best miter box you can get (about $75 and up). The rest of the tools can be picked up out of pocket cash as you need them.

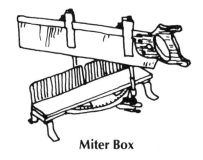

Miter Box

A few jobs that a professional cabinet maker with a shop would do differently than they are done by an amateur with portable hand tools are described twice so that the reader can decide for himself or herself what compromises are involved in doing the job at home. A pro will make a dado (the groove in upright boards that cabinet shelves sit in) in one pass across a table saw. An amateur can do the job with a hand-held circular saw in four passes and fill in any flaws with slivers of wood. The finished shelf will be just as strong. Similarly, drawers can be made at home but the product is clumsy compared to the fairly polished job an amateur can do on the rest of the cabinetry.

Out of the entire kitchen—which is by far the most complicated project you will undertake in renovating an old house—only three jobs should be sublet to someone with shop tools. If you want to trim the formica countertop with wood, you must have the 1×2 passed over a joiner to remove the rounded edges that would collect crumbs where the wood meets the formica. The cost will be a couple of dollars. You should have the drawers built, although you can build the cabinet they sit in and hang them yourself. You might pay to have the dadoes made for the shelves to save time and produce a neater product. If you cut the shelf sides first and mark the needed dadoes, the shop time will be minimal. The few jobs that do require professional help are stripped in the text to the bare minimum that cannot be done at home.

Do your kitchen last. There are so many criteria to make a successful kitchen that a year or two of designing is a bare minimum. If you find a place for elbows, a place for the coffee-filter cone that doesn't compete with anything else, and a place to chop your vegetables without turning your back on guests, you have a rare kitchen that will more than make up for any imperfections in craftsmanship.

A complete kitchen rebuild—floors, counters, cabinets, walls, sink and wiring—will take an inexperienced person three weeks full-time with intermittent help. The cost will be a quarter to a half of the cost of an architect-designed kitchen built by a contractor.

Prices are given with some of the projects. Besides giving the book a nice nostalgic glow, they provide some basis for estimating. You must come up with a current percentage figure for

inflation. Lumber prices are tightly linked together; if you find a few prices have gone up 30 percent, you can safely add 30 percent to all wood items. Electrical and plumbing supply prices are subject to large discounts when overstock builds up in warehouses so you should watch the display ads in the newspapers and buy in advance.

Time estimates are also given although they are necessarily rough. These are a sort of thumbnail average of many jobs done by amateurs and run two or three or even four times as long as a pro would take. If a cost estimate isn't given for a job you want to do, the standard rule on renovation is to add up all the materials costs you can find in your plans and double the figure. Triple your first time estimate to account for the heating duct in the wall you didn't know anything about.

The biggest problem in old house renovation is finding the moldings that were offered in much larger selection at the turn of the century. Very recently an array of small companies has sprung up to sell reproduction moldings. The catalog chapter lists a number of these companies to give some idea of what is available and what they cost. These companies will all ship to individual customers in small quantities.

The cabinet doors in this kitchen are redwood tongue-and-groove salvaged from a chicken coop and belt-sanded. When they were glued at the T&G joints and trimmed with dadoed 2x2 that has been glued on they became very stable. Eggshell verathane was painted on both sides of the doors and no stain was used.

For an extensive exterior paint-removal project such as this Victorian scaffolding is necessary.

Moldings are expensive but used in small quantities they can make new work feel like the original. If your intention is precise restoration, you will probably have to have your moldings made to order by a production molding shop. This usually involves a grinding fee for shaper blades to mill the wood (about $50) as well as the cost of materials and labor. If close is good enough, you may find something that will do in the catalog chapter. Ordering and shipping instructions are included.

A sample of hardware suppliers is listed although only a suggestion of their lines could be printed. You will have to send for their catalogs or buy off the shelf, using the illustrations only for purposes of getting ideas and estimating.

Modern materials are recommended in the text where these are clearly superior to the period treatment. Formica is the easiest countertop to pay for and live with and can be installed with special tools costing less than $15. Steel drawer guides greatly simplify the placement of kitchen drawers and provide a smoother acting drawer than can be had with wooden guides. Plastic resin oil finishes are recommended because they are painted on with a brush, allowed to seep, then wiped away with rags, leaving only the finish that has penetrated into the wood and eliminating problems with runs or dust. Because refinishing old wood and matching mixed species of wood are a big part of renovating an old house, a chapter is devoted to paint stripping, staining and finishing wood.

The emphasis in The Blue Thumb Guide is on low-budget operations retaining as much as possible of the original, recycling where feasible, and using only hand tools. You will also need one of the excellent home maintenance textbooks for jobs that can only be done in the standard manner. Instructions for hanging wallpaper, for instance, are not given because they are so readily available elsewhere. Stippling is explained instead, and might provide an attractive alternative at 5 percent the cost. Stippling came into vogue after World War I and its use on the walls of a Victorian house is anach-

This entire house was built in three months by two people who had only occasional help. The flooring came from a barn and was left rough-hewn. Other lumber was bought from a local mill in mixed batches called "farmer's loads." All the doors and windows were salvaged from other sites with the exception of the octagonal picture window which was built according to the simple plans in chapter five and cost $65. Other windows in the house were constructed from glazier's scraps and leaded together. The total cost—without figuring land and utility hook-ups but including wiring, plumbing and a refrigerator—was $7,000.

ronistic. You are involved in a trade-off: wallpaper is expensive; embossed wallpaper, which is authentic, is geometrically more expensive. Stippling can give you the feel you are after on a tight budget.

If you are broke from the down payment but full of energy, start on the walls. Your first attempt at wallboard and taping compound will turn out perfectly because you can keep going over it until it does. If you get all the walls finished and are still broke, start on the floors. In three days of hard work you can refinish the entire upstairs regardless of the condition the wood is in. The cost is under $200, which is less than the cost of carpeting a single room.

Many people contributed to this book, among them several who have become so involved in the art of personalized housing that they have devoted full-time to it as freelance craftsmen. I am especially indebted to Tom Ward of Petaluma, California, whose work appears frequently in this book. Tom has a genius for spontaneous design that elevates his work to an art. In Seattle, I have spent many hours at the dinner table of Kathy and Ernst Kaemke discussing such topics as the best length for a tape measure and why carpenters always rest their elbows on their knees when they take a break. Steve Whitney, Larkin McAllister and Henry Ely, all of San Francisco, contributed shortcuts and projects.

Photographs came from the homes of people who were kind enough to allow me to take pictures: Doug Montgomery of San Francisco; Steve Whittacker of Shelton, Washington; Ruth and Vic Quinet, Mary and John Sweeney, Richard and Julie Zahler, of Seattle; Lester Hawkins, Carol Grover and Bill Moffett of Occidental, California; Jane and Lee Mizrahi, of Sebastopol, California.

The drawings, except those of tools, were done by John de Lorimier, a muralist living in Bodega Bay, California. I traced the tools out of dealers' catalogs with a rapidograph. Amy Solomon helped with preparation of the manuscript.

This book is for Ernst and Kathy Kaemke.

HOUSING STYLES: LOOKING AT WHAT YOU HAVE

This is a very general guide to the style of your house. Though it may not necessarily look just like any one of these styles, by looking at the elements you'll be able to figure out the main influences the builder was under when your house was constructed. Architecture often reflects the philosophy of its era: by the turn of the century the Romanticism that built the Victorians had begun to give way to the Rationalism of the twentieth century—that is, the same philosophy that built the Model T.

The façade of your house belongs to the street. If the exterior is even vaguely recognizable as an architectural style—even one that is not currently popular—you do your neighbors a disservice when you disrupt it. Elaborate trim and fancy bannisters tacked to the front of a 1920s bungalow will soon be viewed the way we now look at plywood additions to the fronts of Victorians.

The most pleasant way to establish what trim detail might have been removed from your façade is to walk around the neighborhood and search for similar buildings. Urban libraries often carry architects' catalogs of housing plans going back to the 1920s. Reprints of catalogs from the Victorian period are popular and can usually be found filed in the art section of the library.

Gothic Revival style is distinguished by the pointed arch on the windows and doors. The roof is usually steeply pitched with tall chimneys and asymmetrical gables. Fanciwork may decorate the eaves and windows. The house is usually surfaced

Gothic Revival

in one material and painted one color and its general appearance is quaint rather than formal. These houses were popular as early as the 1700s and led the Romantic revival just before the Victorian era. They were also built after World War I.

Victorian encompasses a group of houses built after the Civil War but before World War I. Massing (the arrangement of the volume of the house) is vertical, even when the house sits on a large lot. There are often eccentric displays of gingerbread. Classic columns are combined with fish-scale shingles and a wide variety of textures and materials on the siding. Very late models might have a living room but most had a large hallway leading to many very small rooms. Symmetrical bay windows with plain or elaborate scrollwork belong to the *Italianate Victorian*. Round towers mark one form of the *Queen Anne*. Very elaborate façades are indicative of the *Carpenter Gothic* style. The use of wood turned on a lathe characterizes the *Eastlake Victorian*.

The *Shingle style* house is a plain boxy structure with shingles painted, aged or stained a dark color. Windows are usually double-hung and set with many small panes, flush with the wall. Shutters are common, but decoration is usually minimal except for some detailing at the entrance.

The *Elizabethan* house is characterized by exposed half-timbers on the second story with the area between filled with stucco. Leaded windows are typical and at least some portion of the upper story overhangs the first, providing a larger living space on the second floor. Beamed ceilings and massive woodwork mark the interiors. The house is asymmetrical; any kind

Queen Anne

Italianate

Shingle Style

Elizabethan

of material may have been used to cover the lower façade.

The *English Cottage* is a low, one-and-a-half-story house with a sharply peaked roof and dormers making bedrooms in the attic possible. The exterior may be made of a variety of materials but the house is usually dominated by an oversized chimney on the front or side. The design is purposefully quaint even at the expense of space inside. Windows may be elaborate but are set usually in simple frames.

English Cottage

The *Bungalow* is a generic name for a widely varying type of house built from 1900 through 1920 and ranging in style from simple boxes to larger two-story houses with Swiss or Japanese influences. Large overhanging eaves are common in rainy climates and are often supported by large brackets. The double-hung windows are plain or plain below with a decorated sash above. A porch typically encloses the entire front of the house; porch pillars are square and rise from a closed porch railing. The treatment of the exterior may be of a variety of materials but is usually finished with white trim on a dark background. Heavy woodwork marks the more elaborate interiors. In its simplest form the bungalow isn't much more than a box and nearly any sort of remodeling will be in keeping so long as the lines are simple.

International is the name applied to the products of the Rationalist school of architecture. The roofs are flat; extensive glass is used. The few interior walls are very plain partitions. The exterior walls are also as plain as possible and often use stucco or reinforced concrete. Frank Lloyd Wright called his invention *a roof over a volume, with a view.* Le Corbusier saw it as *a machine for living in.* The mass-produced versions are the split-level ranch houses often decorated with other influences and called by other names (such as "Colonial" when columns were added to the front porch).

Colonial is the style that was most frequently built between the two World Wars. Variations abound but most of these houses are symmetrical and often have dormers piercing the steep roof. Working shutters were a common addition. The exterior was usually of shiplap painted white. The entrance is usually centered and bay windows aren't uncommon. The sizes of these houses vary from small, story-and-a-half cottages to pillared Southern mansions.

Colonial

Georgian

The *Georgian* is a symmetrical, nearly cubical house that is normally large with a flat roof or one that slopes from the center to all four eaves. Though traditionally of stone or brick, wooden exteriors are seen—sometimes with heavy wood inserts at the corners meant to suggest stone quoins that are used to protect the corners of brick houses. Chimneys are usually placed at both ends of the house and the entrance may be plain or columned.

The *Regency* is similar to the Georgian in massing, with matching windows on both sides of the door repeated on the first and second stories. Shutters may line the windows and there may be only one chimney. The decoration is usually less extensive and less traditional than on the Georgian. When

Regency

Western Row House

there's more detailing on windows and a cast-iron balustrade circling a flat roof the style is called *Federal*. A roof that slopes at a very steep angle to a second much flatter roof and is pierced by a dormer window is called *Mansard*. French doors and iron fretwork often complete the Mansard variation.

The *Western Row House* is distinguished by its common side walls that link each with its neighbor. Post World War I versions are often stuccoed and trimmed with wrought iron and rounded arches, showing a Spanish or Moorish influence. Western row houses were often single-family dwellings of two or three stories; façades varied to increase the appearance of a separation of the units. Bay windows commonly grace the fronts to compensate for the lack of side windows.

The *Brownstone* is so called because it's commonly surfaced with a type of sandstone by that name. These Eastern urban houses are often of four or five stories and were once divided into apartments using a common front door. There is a widespread Brownstone renovation movement of late, and many are being restored to their single-family status. Brownstones may span an entire block; where the block is divided into separate buildings, they share a common wall. Flat roofs and double-hung windows are typical.

Brownstone

TOOLS: THOSE YOU NEED (AND THOSE YOU DON'T)

This list of tools isn't exhaustive, and it's the kind of list that no two people agree upon. But this tool list works for me and it will help you. If you're working on your own house on a limited budget, pick your projects according to what you can afford and build your collection of tools as you go. The tools that are listed in this chapter are the basic ones that you'll need frequently for the whole range of projects that face you in an older house. More specialized tools are explained in the text as they are needed so you can wait to buy them.

Buy the cheapest *screwdrivers* you can get. Buy them by the dozen. Screwdrivers are like cups of sugar: your friends will borrow them without a thought that they ought to give them back. Screwdrivers have legs.

Other than the cheapest possible, the only screwdrivers to buy would be *Sears Craftsman*, on sale. *Craftsman* tools are high quality and expensive, but sales are frequent and the mark-down brings them in line with the cheaper makes. Sears also has a policy of replacing any of their hand tools at any store without a cash register receipt regardless of the reason the tool failed—a policy I've tested and appreciated.

Screwdrivers come in a variety of sizes to match the size of the slot in the screw head. It is important that the screwdriver fit the slot and fill it completely to its bottom, or the force won't be evenly spread and you take a chance of shaving the metal off the shoulders of the slot and destroying the screw. When this happens, you'll have to drill the screw out, starting with a tiny drill bit and working your way outward in stages until you have eaten the screw away. This is a lot of work, so use the right screwdriver in the first place to avoid having to do it.

If the blade of the screwdriver gets so blunted that it doesn't fill the slot snugly to the bottom, sharpen it slightly with two or three passes with a file. Don't take away too much or it will meet the slot only at the edges and will ruin the head.

The proper-sized hole for the screw is the width of the shank —so that the threads have material to engage. For small screws, this is simple. For large screws, especially going into hardwood, as many as three drilling operations are necessary. (See below under *drill bits*.) When working with hardwood, it's well worth your while to rub hand soap on the screw threads for lubrication.

Hammers are rated by the weight of the head and the quality of the handle. They are catagorized according to the job they are made to do.

Buy yourself a good 16-oz. *claw hammer* for general home renovation. The cheap $5 models aren't heavy enough to drive a nail without wearing you out. The more blows you have to make, the more chance you have of banging up either the wood or your fingers.

Heavier *framing hammers* with long handles are for pounding 16-penny nails. If you are doing a good deal of framing, a heavy hammer is a justifiable luxury.

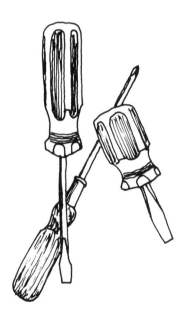

Get yourself plenty of cheap screwdrivers–they disappear.

When pulling nails, use a block of wood as a fulcrum between the hammerhead and the working surface once the nail is 1½ inches or so out of the wood. The hammer will have much greater pulling power with less strain on the handle.

A wedge can be driven into the head of a wood-handled hammer if the handle comes loose. Soaking the hammer in a bucket of water overnight will do the same job temporarily though the handle will loosen again when the wood dries out. The foam rubber grips on steel-handled hammers begin to slip with time. Fiberglass handles are eventually jolted loose by vibration and aren't so easily repaired as wood handles.

When a hammer gets old, the striking surface sometimes becomes rounded, causing it to bend nails even with a good blow. A grinding wheel will flatten the surface again. Be sure to round off the edges slightly to minimize the damage done when you miss your nail.

You don't need a *rubber mallet* often but they're cheap. They can usually be found in a sale tool bin at hardware stores. You must use a rubber mallet when striking a wood-handled chisel and one should be used on plastic-handled tools which will eventually shatter even if you use the side of a steel hammer head to strike them. The mallets made of white rubber don't mar furniture; the cheap black ones do.

Rubber Mallet

Always use a *nailset* on finishing nails that will show to avoid the final hammer blow that leaves the mark when you try to set the nail flush. With a nailset, you can recess the head of the finishing nail slightly to allow puttying for a fine job. Always putty nail holes *after* you apply the stain and finish or the putty will fill the soft grain of the wood and alter the way it accepts finish. There is no good way of getting rid of an ugly putty blotch except by scraping and sanding the wood away and starting over.

Nail Set

Another tool that looks exactly like a nailset but has a pointed tip is a center punch and is used to make a dimple in metal so the drill bit won't squirrel around while getting started. If you mistake this for a nailset, it will slide off the nail and gouge the wood. Nailsets are sold in cardboard racks usually on the counter of hardware stores near the cash register for under $2.

A single ¾-inch or 1-inch *chisel* will do just about every job you need a chisel for. If you chip the chisel blade by hitting a nail, by dropping it on a concrete floor or by using it to open cans of paint, make a new edge on a grinding wheel or belt-sander. Tool steel is very hard, so work slowly, giving the blade plenty of time to cool. If you get it hot enough to turn blue, you will lose the temper or hardness of the steel and the blade won't stay sharp. A piece of 100-grit or finer sandpaper placed flat on a table will sharpen a chisel. Use a pushing motion and take care to hold the angle of the blade so that the full beveled edge touches the sandpaper.

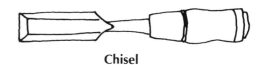

Chisel

The blade of a chisel has a flat side and a beveled side which gets the sharpening. In wood, the chisel will tend to follow the direction of the bevel, so keep this side down while chiseling. An upside-down chisel will want to dig down into the wood rather than lifting a layer of wood evenly.

Jack Plane

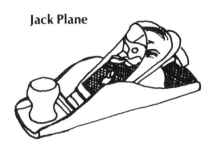

The *jack plane* is used for making saw-cut edges even and planing down wood that is slightly oversized but isn't enough so to saw. You only occasionally have a job fine enough to require planed fitting but when you do the work is the most satisfying you can run across.

What you're able to design will be largely determined by the dimension of the lumber available to you. If you don't have a cabinetshop available to cut custom sizes, you'll quickly covet milled edges. With a jack plane you can mill your own straight enough to show although not usually straight enough to accept trim.

If you can't afford twenty dollars for a larger plane, make do with a six dollar 6-inch Stanley or one like it. It will bevel the edges on new-sawn boards with enough accuracy to smooth nicely with sandpaper. On some boards, it will even plane a long edge with accuracy.

Almost all planes use friction blade adjustments. The blade is a flat piece of tool steel backed by stiffener made of heavier metal and sometimes by an adjusting lever. A turn-screw holds the blade and the stiffener in the bed in the body of the plane.

Adjusting the blade is tricky and takes some patience. Turn the plane upside down and sight along the sole, or bottom. When the blade is 1/16th inch exposed and level from left to right, tighten the turn-screw. The blade will move out of alignment. Try again.

Never lay a plane flat on its sole or you'll dull the blade.

Handsaws are identified by the number of teeth they have per inch. An 8-point handsaw has eight teeth per inch and is used for ripping along the direction of the grain. A 10-point handsaw is for cutting across the grain. If you will have only one handsaw, get a 10-point. Most of your ripping will be done with a circular saw.

45°

A dull saw of any kind will pull to the side and take a long time to complete a cut and do a bad job. If your saw does this, take it to a saw shop and have the teeth straightened and sharpened. The cost is under $5.

You'll get straighter cuts both ripping and cross-cutting if you hold the saw at a 45 degree angle to the wood. The blade is guided by the cut it has already made, called the kerf. At 45 degrees, the saw has enough kerf to guide it but isn't so close to the wood that it grinds away at parts that it is not yet cutting.

Saw in both directions—pushing away and pulling back toward you—without bearing down too hard. Rust adds friction, so keep the blade oiled and rust-free.

A *backsaw* is a saw with a stiffened spine used for fine cutting. This saw comes with most miter boxes and is rarely used except in them. Part of what you pay when you buy a good miter box is the price of a good quality backsaw.

There is a very wide variety of specialty saws that you will need rarely but badly when you do. Coping saws, hacksaws and keyhole saws can be had from the sale tool bin. The quality is low but you will use these saws rarely. Most of their functions can be performed with a saber saw.

Coping Saw

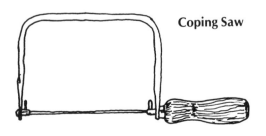

A *coping saw* has a blade about ¼ inch deep that can turn tight circles because there isn't enough depth to the blade to be restricted by the saw kerf. It has a high-arched frame stretching the blade taut. The frame is far enough from the blade to allow you to cut 6 to 8 inches into the board and make gingerbread cutouts. If you have more than a little job, buy several extra blades. Blades break easily but are cheap. There's no reason to wear yourself out with a dull blade.

To make a cutout without cutting the edge of the board, drill a hole, remove the blade from the saw, run it through the hole and hook it back up.

A *keyhole saw* has a wider blade than a coping saw but is also used for cutting curves. The blade is tapered from handle to tip so that the tip can turn sharply while the handle end is controlled by the kerf already cut. A keyhole saw can't cut as tight a circle as a coping saw, but its cut is smoother. As the keyhole saw has no frame, it can cut to the interior of any width material.

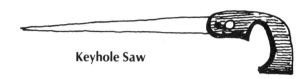

Keyhole Saw

A *hacksaw* is used for cutting metal. It has a frame similar to that of the coping saw, with the blade stretched between the two ends. Use cutting oil or another light oil to cut down friction when sawing metal; replace the blades often. Sawing is accomplished on the down stroke with a hacksaw. Release the pressure on the backstroke or you will quickly dull your blade.

Shaped-sheet metal, like gutters, is cut with a hacksaw to avoid bending the metal. Most other sheet metal, like flashing, is cut with heavy-duty scissors, called tin snips.

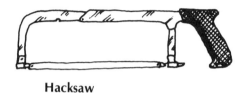

Hacksaw

Get a 16-foot *steel measuring tape*. It's more expensive than the shorter lengths and the case is 2½ inches long which is inconvenient on inside measurements, but this tape will measure the whole wall on most rooms and do shorter jobs as well as a shorter tape. If you look every time you get near a sale tool bin, you should be able to pick up a cheap 50-foot tape.

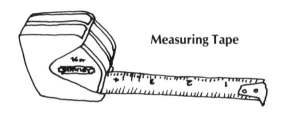

Measuring Tape

You use a *combination square* so often that it's worth your while to get a good one although the cheap models do an adequate job. Combination squares have fixed settings for 90° and 45° and are used for all cutting that isn't done in a miter box. A *framing square* is much larger and is used for truing up cabinets, walls and steps.

Get the best *miter box* you can get your hands on. The trick in finish carpentry is to hide all large joints but eventually when you get down to moldings the joints show. The cheapest miter boxes that will do a consistently adequate job start at about $75. The $4 wooden ones aren't worth taking home. The saw is guided by a factory-cut kerf which is inadequate when it's new and very quickly becomes sloppy as the saw chews away at it. Stanley, which normally produces excellent tools including miter boxes, also produces a line of toy miter boxes. If you pay $140 and get a Miller Falls miter box, you'll have an heirloom and your joints will fit.

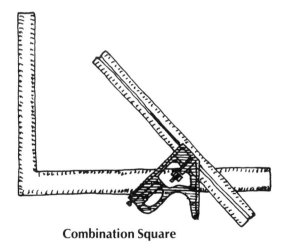

Combination Square

Unless you're pouring concrete or doing new construction, a *level* is of little value to you. It is more important that your work line up with existing ceilings and floors than be level.

Chalk lines are handy for cutting plywood or plasterboard. A piece of blue chalk and a string will do the job.

Pipe clamps (also called pony clamps) are the most versatile clamps available at about $6 plus pipe. One end of the clamp screws onto the threaded end of a piece of plumbing pipe. The other end slides on the pipe for adjustment. The clamp will accept any size project shorter than the pipe. Pipe clamps are made to fit ½- and ¾-inch galvanized plumbing pipe so you must know what pipe you will use before buying.

When using pipe clamps to glue edging on plywood or particle board, use a 2×4 on edge to distribute the pressure evenly and avoid bowing the strip. On smaller jobs any smooth scrap of wood will serve to prevent clamp marks.

C Clamp

C-clamps don't have wide enough jaws to be of much use in gluing unless you are laying pieces face-to-face to strengthen a shelf, but they are very useful for clamping guides. These can sometimes be picked up at rummage sales or stores that carry used tools. C-clamps are the sort of tool you pick up when you can at garage sales.

Cheap power tools will do the job as well as better ones but they are slower. A $20 circular saw will eventually get you to the end of a long cut in a piece of plywood, but your cut will be much straighter if you slide a better saw along at a natural pace and avoid fatigue which is a real factor in the quality of your work.

Circular Saw

As *circular saws* go up in price, the horsepower increases and the bearings get better. A $125 circular saw is a true joy. A $40 saw is adequate for all your needs, up to and including building a house from scratch.

If you are working in a site without electricity, a $12 voltage converter does a surprisingly good job of providing electricity to power tools. The tools must be rated for direct current (many are) and the vehicle must have an alternator instead of a generator.

The proper blade is important to good work with a circular saw. Use the cheap combination blade that comes with the saw as a junk blade for cutting old wood or flooring or plaster. A good carbon-tipped combination blade will do most of the rest of the jobs. For fine cutting plywood, get a teflon-coated fine-toothed plywood blade. This is slower than a combination blade but makes a cabinet-work quality cut. Metal cutting blades are available and work very well.

Power Drill

Always saw with the face of your work up and the blade set to project about ¼ inch through the wood. If both sides of the cut are crucial, clamp a piece of scrap on the bottom side to minimize torn grain. When a blade begins to pull to either side, it is dull and should be replaced or sharpened (about $4).

Power drills are separated by the size of the chuck, the size of the motor, and whether or not the drill features reverse drive and variable speed control. Reverse drive is of no value unless you have a couple hundred screws to remove but variable speed is useful. You want slow speeds for drilling metal or synthetics and higher speeds for polishing, buffing or grinding.

Quarter-inch drills will accept any bit or attachment up to ¼ inch in diameter and are usually geared very fast to make up for the small motors that run them. These are adequate for most home wood projects and can be gotten for under $20.

If you will have only one drill, a ⅜-inch drill will accept a larger range of bits and broaden the range of projects you are able to undertake. These are usually geared lower to produce more torque but fewer RPMs and are actually less useful than the cheaper units for buffing. You can get a good one for $40.

Because so many projects require the use of more than one bit and changing bits is time consuming, two drills—a good ⅜- and a cheap ¼-inch—are an excellent idea as soon as your tool collection has grown sufficiently to allow such luxury.

Variable speed drills go slow enough to drive screws and the salesman will probably make a big deal of this. In fact, in a direct drive arrangement, there is no place for the equipment to slip except at the screw head which means that you will ruin as many screws as you place. A special clutch arrangement (about $4) fits into the chuck and gives you much better control. This is an absolute necessity if you wish to drive screws with your drill.

You don't need high quality *drill bits* except for drilling metal and you will save money by buying these one at a time as you need them. To keep the drill bit from squirrelling around the metal, use a centering punch to make a dimple and start the drill bit. Be sure to use plenty of cutting or sewing machine oil when drilling metal, and the slowest speed possible. You should be producing distinct metal shavings. If you aren't, you are going too fast. Cheap ¼-inch drills do a poor job on metal because of their high speed.

For drilling wood, cheap bits do a fine job. These are broken and lost so consistently that good ones, which are harder and more brittle, are a poor day-to-day choice. In a pinch, a finishing nail or box nail with the head clipped off will make a fine drill bit.

Larger screws or screws going into hardwoods require a three-step hole: a pilot hole which extends to the desired depth; a larger hole for the shank of the screw; and a countersink to accept the head so that the flathead screw will pull down flush. If you leave out any of these three steps, the screw will either split the wood or refuse to sit down neatly. Combination bits do all three jobs at once but must be bought to match the screw. A set of these (about $5) is a real time-saver.

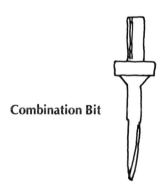

Combination Bit

Shovel Bit

Shovel bits are considerably cheaper than twist drill bits in larger sizes. A set of these ranging from ⅜ to 1 inch is a good buy. These work well in softwoods but have a tendency to tear the wood as they pass through it. If the backside of the hole matters, clamp a piece of scrap to it or stop drilling as soon as the point passes through the wood and finish the hole from the other side.

There is more *junk* sold to augment a power hand drill than any other tool. Buffers and grinding wheels are usually sold in a set and are sometimes useful and cheap. Shaper heads, meant to make the drill double as a router will do an adequate job on a very light rounding. These can be used to round a newly ripped board to match the rounded edge which comes on factory milled lumber. You can do the job as rapidly by hand with sandpaper.

In the *total junk* department are a number of attachments that don't do anything at all but which look like they will. These are manufactured only because enough new people come into the market each year to be fooled, once.

Drill stands made to convert a hand drill into a drill press top the list. When the bit touches the wood, it shifts the drill even in the best of these, giving you an approximately placed hole. You can do as well by hand and save $20 and a lot of set-up time. If you have a need for a drill press, a real one can be rented from a tool rental shop for about five dollars a day. The bench model will fit in your car.

There is an attachment made to convert a power drill into a *circular saw*. This attachment should be illegal. Underpowered tools are very dangerous because they tend to bind and throw either the tool or the stock.

Rotary rasps, a sort of metal grinding wheel, are sold for use in drills. You can do a faster and neater job with a hand rasp which has enough surface area to produce a neat job.

A *saber saw*, also called a jig saw, is one of the most effective cheap tools available. Equipped with the right blade, it will cut metal, wood, formica, pipe or just about anything, replacing a variety of specialty hand saws. A $15 saber saw will do anything if you are patient enough. A good two-speed or variable-speed model will run about $30 and is worth the extra money. Use higher speeds for cutting lumber, plywood and compositions, lower speeds for metal and pipe. Blades break frequently so a quantity should be kept on hand.

Power sanders come in three types: orbital; disk and belt. *Orbital sanders* vibrate very rapidly in either an oval pattern or straight back and forth. Some models can be set for either motion. These are used for polishing and are of little value for stripping old paint or removing wood. They will take a very long time to remove a scratch from a piece of furniture. You can do anything an orbital sander can do as quickly with a sanding block powered by hand.

Disk sanders range from light-weight attachments for power drills up to heavy-duty models useful for preparing the outside of your house for paint or for working fiberglass. These must be kept in motion at all times or they will dig into the wood. As the sandpaper moves in a circular motion, it is impossible to keep it running with the grain of the wood, which makes a disk sander a poor choice for final sanding on wood which will take a natural finish. Sandpaper disks are much cheaper than belts

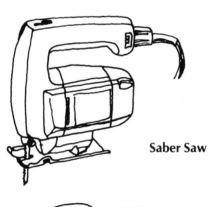

Saber Saw

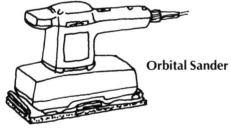

Orbital Sander

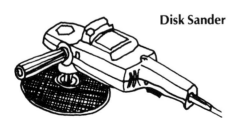

Disk Sander

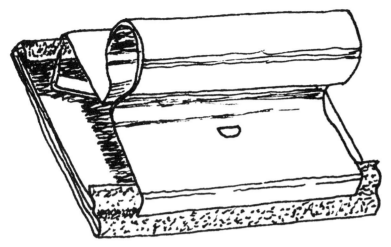

Patent Sanding Block

which makes this tool more economical than a belt sander for large jobs. Most disk sanders are arranged so that the sandpaper is bolted in place. Some are designed to have the sandpaper glued onto the shoe with contact cement. The cement holds the paper tightly on the edges, which is not the case with bolted paper. The paper lasts longer and peels off easily for replacement. The glued paper system can be used with special blades on a table saw or circular saw for sanding endgrain. The long edge of a board can't be passed along the blade.

Belt sanders are more expensive to operate than disk sanders and are a poor choice for cleaning up old paint on the shiplap façade of a house because the belts will catch and tear on the shiplap above the one being worked. Because the belt moves in one direction, belt sanders are the best choice for finishing wood where the grain will show. These are powerful enough to take down scratches in furniture quickly or to mill rough wood and are probably the best choice in power sanders for versatility if you can afford the stiff ($50-100) price.

Sandpaper is graded by the number of grits per square inch with the lower numbers indicating coarser grades. Use the same grade paper regardless of the machine you are using or whether you are sanding by hand. The 25-40 grit is very coarse, to be used for rapid removal of old finish or for cleaning up very rough wood. The 60-80 grit is an intermediate grade for taking out the scratches left by the coarser grades. It will produce a surface smooth enough for paint. Finish sandpaper —100-120 grit—will produce a surface ready to be oiled or varnished. The finest grades, 400-600 grit, are used for wet-sanding by hand to produce a hand-rubbed finish. Lubricated with finish, wet-sanding will quickly produce an extremely smooth finish.

Hand-sanding goes quickly on cabinet jobs using new lumber. Change your paper often, whenever the grit begins to fill in with debris. Greater detail on sanding and finishing is given in the chapter on refinishing.

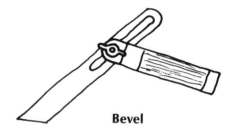

Bevel

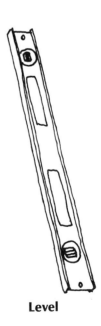

Level

WALLS AND FLOORS: AN EASY START AND FINISH

If you've just bought the house and are short of cash but anxious to get started working you can always begin on the walls. Except for papering, which is expensive, wall work is the easiest renovation project of all. The results are dramatic and your first try will come out well because you keep at it until it does.

Most older houses have walls of lath and plaster. Lath—rough sawn strips of wood about ⅜ by 2 inches—was nailed to the studs horizontally with ¼-inch gaps. Plaster—mixed with fiber to give it tensile strength and allowing it to expand and contract—was spread over the lath, filling the gaps so the finished wall had a good grip on the wood.

Where only small areas of the plaster are bad, you can repair them with Spackle or wallboard compound. Both are available in powder form or premixed with liquid; the premixed is much more convenient and slightly more expensive. Spackle is more versatile than wallboard compound but costs more.

Pick away the plaster that has come loose from the lath with your fingers. Don't get too ambitious or there'll be no stopping. Once started, you can easily tear a sound wall down in large chunks. Be sure to get all loose plaster out, including any buckled sections that curve out from the level of the wall.

Sometimes the edge of the old plaster will be crumbly although it still has a good grip on the lath. A coat of shellac or white glue thinned with water will keep it intact.

If the area you have cleared of rotten plaster is less than a foot across, spray it with water to assure good adhesion and fill it in with wallboard compound. The first filling will shrink as it dries and develop cracks. Allow the patch to dry completely to a light uniform color. This can take as much as a week in the winter time but rushing it will only slow down the drying of later coats of mud.

Spread a second coat of compound to fill the cracks and smooth the patch job. Less compound goes on in this second coat and cracks, therefore, will be much smaller or nonexistent. Three or four coats will be necessary. The last coat is thin and dries in half a day.

You can speed up the drying time of the first thick coat by using Fixall or Durabond 90, both of which set up much faster than wallboard compound and won't produce cracks as they dry. Be sure to work the first coat well into the cracks between the lath. Mix only as much as you'll need; the excess will dry up in the bucket. Both Fixall and Durabond 90 dry too hard to sand and shouldn't be used for finish coats.

Larger sections of rotten plaster will tend to sag if you aren't fast and experienced at wetwall application. A sheet of newspaper can help keep a large section intact. Lay in a coat of mud about half as thick as the finished wall and cover it with a layer of damp newspaper. Punch holes in the newspaper an inch apart with the point of a pocketknife to join the paper and the mud. Be sure not to leave bubbles; cut the newspaper if any occur. Cover with a second coat of mud before the first layer sets.

Dampen the lath before patching the plaster.

Finish the job with wallboard compound in the same manner as on small areas.

If the area of plaster to be redone is large, much over a yard across, clear it down to the lath and put in a piece of wallboard nailed to the studs. This is often necessary in stairwells and hallways where the wall gets a lot of traffic and jostling.

You'll quickly find out that the thickness of the old plaster is not even. Shim the plasterboard with whatever is available—thin strips of wood shaved from a scrap with a pocket knife, folded empty matchbook covers—until you have it even in thickness with the plaster around the edge of the area to be repaired.

Tape the cracks between the old plaster and new wallboard as you would new plasterboard, laying down a coat of plasterboard compound, a strip of paper-joint tape, then another coat of compound. The joint tape adds strength to the joint.

The finished wall will have wows in it. Feather these out and away from the joint with a broad wood-backed taping knife. The wooden spine will keep the blade from cupping as you taper the irregularity out over the widest possible area. Holding the broadknife perpendicular to the wall will further reduce the blade's tendency to cup under pressure.

Before raking yourself over the coals for an imperfect job, take a close look at your other walls. There is no such thing as a perfectly straight lath-and-plaster wall; there are only walls where the variation is not so abrupt that it is visible.

Some walls were papered with wallpaper as the original treatment. These often lack the final skim coat that was used to finish walls that were intended for painting. Peel off as much wallpaper as you can with your fingernails or with the aid of a pancake turner or broadknife. If you're lucky, the paper will come off in large sheets, especially if several coats of paper are present. If large areas of wallpaper remain, rent a wallpaper steamer from a tool rental outfit and steam them off.

If only small sections of wallpaper are left, coat these with wallboard compound. The moisture will loosen the glue so these final areas can be stripped.

Once the wallpaper is gone, give the wall a skim coat of wallboard compound, scraping off as much as you can as you go to avoid building high spots. The first skim coat will have flaws caused by sand which comes loose from the original plaster and gets caught under your blade.

Allow the skim coat to dry (30 minutes to an hour is usually long enough), sand it quickly with medium-grit sandpaper to knock away loose particles, and give the wall a final skim coat. The result will be a smooth wall ready for priming and painting.

New wallboard is often the answer where the old wall is in very poor condition or is simply ugly under coats of wallpaper and years of nail holes. Wallboard—also called *gypsum board*, *drywall* or *sheetrock*—is plaster of Paris with a paper coating on both sides to provide tensile strength and a reasonably durable finish. It is strong enough to do away with the layer of wooden lath that was necessary when wet walls were made on the spot.

The first layer of mud will crack as it dries.

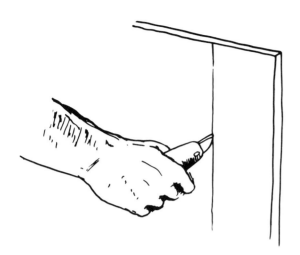

Slit the back of the wallboard and then bend it until the plaster snaps so that it can be shaped to the surface.

Wallboard is easy to work with. A special razor knife (about $2) is used to slit through the paper on one side through part of the thickness of the plaster along the intended cut. The sheet of wallboard is then bent away from the cut side until the plaster breaks. The paper on the backside is slit and the cut is complete.

Wallboard is nailed up with special ringed nails that will not slip once they are pounded into the stud. The idea is to set the nail slightly below the surface level of the wallboard without breaking the paper. To do this the final hammer blow should create a small depression which can be filled in with wallboard compound during the taping to cover the nailhead.

Nails which break through the paper coating have no holding power. If you bend a nail and it starts to rip the paper surface of the wallboard, pull it out using a block of wood to protect the wallboard from the head of the hammer during the pulling and start again with a new nail.

Old fir studs are often so hard that it is difficult to drive ringed wallboard nails into them. If nail bending is a problem, go to heavier roofing nails.

If the old lath and plaster is in poor shape under the new wallboard, you may have to use double nailing to be sure that the wallboard fits tightly. Drive two nails in tandem about 3 inches apart, alternating blows between them to slowly pull

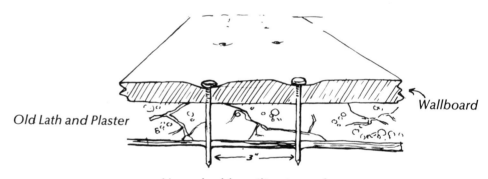

Old Lath and Plaster

Wallboard

Use a double nailing to apply wallboard over a lath-and-plaster wall that has deteriorated.

the wallboard tightly to the stud. Double nailing keeps the strain off any one nail and helps keep the wallboard from springing back which would pull the nailhead under the paper surface.

Measure carefully for outlets and lightswitches and draw the shape of the box on the front of the wallboard. Cut the surface paper with the razor knife, poke a nail through the four corners to mark the cutout and slit the backside. The hole will knock out with taps from a hammer.

Cut the hole ¼ inch higher and lower than the box size to make room for the bolts which will hold the cover plate to the box.

A saber saw does a faster job than the knife on electric box cutouts. Tilt the saw so the end of the blade just touches the wallboard in the middle of the area to be cut. Bear down until the blade sinks through the wallboard and cut out for the box. The paper will be left slightly ragged but this will be covered by the plate.

If the hole is slightly oversized or out of place, it's no catastrophe; you can patch the error while you're taping the seams. Compound alone won't hold; use a strip of perf tape and feather the job as you would a seam. Oversized cover plates are also available to cover oversized holes.

For tall rooms 10- and 12-foot lengths of wallboard are available although they are not always easy to find. If you can locate them, they'll save you taping.

Waterproof wallboard is also available and should be used around bathtubs and shower stalls. It is not necessary to use waterproof wallboard elsewhere in a bathroom but it is crucial that you prime the walls with a waterproof sealer before you paint them. Steam will get at the plastering compound at the joints and nailholes and turn a good job shoddy in a matter of months, if it's not properly sealed. In very humid climates or along the waterfront, all walls should be primed with waterproof sealer.

Wallboard the ceiling first. Occasionally you'll find that there is no joist at the edge of the ceiling and putting up the walls second will allow you to jam the wallboard on the wall tight against the new ceiling to hold it in place.

Wallboard screws can also help in a pinch by allowing you to screw the new wallboard into the old lath if there's no stud where you need it. The joint that results is not as strong as one nailed to the studs. Wallboard screws are driven by an electric hand drill and are often used by pros instead of nails because it's faster.

For nailing on the ceiling build a "T" of 2×4s to help hold the plasterboard in place. The T should be 4 inches or so shorter than the height of the ceiling. The plasterboard will hang down at one end, with the T acting as a fulcrum and its weight will push the other end firmly up against the ceiling for nailing. Nail the wallboard every foot or so around its perimeter, working from one end to the other so you don't bow the plasterboard. Nailing the four corners and working toward the center could cause buckling. Draw two lines down the center using a chalkline or straight edge and nail into the two joists.

Position the wallboard so that it has two joists running down its center. Don't hesitate to chew up the old ceiling a bit to locate the joists so the line can be drawn.

Put up the walls with the sheets of wallboard either horizontally or vertically so long as the edges fall in the center of the studs. Seams will hold up spanning across the 16-inch gap between studs but they will not stand longer throws without being nailed to wood.

If your wallboard does not come out at a stud, cut it back to a stud that it can hit. If there is no stud handy for a long seam,

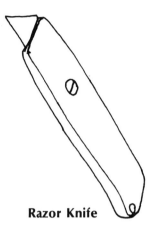

Razor Knife

Use a T made of 2x4s that stands approximately 4 inches shorter than the height of the room to hold the wallboard up while you nail it to the ceiling. One end will sag forcing the other to jam up tightly while you hammer.

Bend the romex into an S shape before attaching the socket or switch so that it will tend to compress easily into the box as you set it.

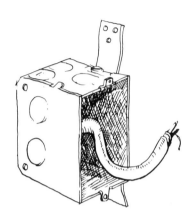

This room has new wallboard walls set over the old studs. The ceiling plaster was left intact and the cracks filled with mud.

tear out some lath and put one in. Use wallboard screws into lath only as a last resort.

If you want to add additional electrical sockets, remove enough plaster to pull out two or three pieces of lath in a horizontal strip at plug-in height. Try to leave a couple inches of plaster above the kickboard so the new wallboard has a foundation consistent with the rest of the wall. The plaster can be cut loose by hand with a chisel or by using a circular saw equipped with an old blade.

Remove the lath and drill a ¾-inch hole in all studs that fall in the path of the wiring. Use 12-gauge romex for plugs and switches, bringing it down from the attic between studs or up from the basement. Romex must be nailed in place with cable staples.

All sockets and switches are placed in wall socket boxes which are made to contain the wires if they come loose from the fixture. Boxes can be had designed to nail in almost any conceivable position—to studs, or to wallboard. Instructions for nailing them in position are included. The wire should enter the box with 6 or 8 inches to spare bent in an S-shape. When the outlet or light switch is installed, the S-shape will be compressed, allowing the element to set back easily into the box.

If you lose any large areas of plaster while stringing the romex, nail scrap lath along the studs to shim them out even with the surface of the old wall. The new wallboard will cover the carnage.

Laying plasterboard over the old wall involves removing the trim but saves a major debris hauling operation. A garbage can half-filled with plaster chunks is a heavy load for two people and the plaster from a single room will fill a pickup truck. Not all dumps will accept plaster because the lime is caustic. Call to find out before you go.

Remove wooden molding from the room, the picture hang-ing strip, the pot-belly molding on top of the kickplate and the trim around windows and doors. Old wood is brittle so pry gently at each nail when removing it. In most cases the nail will stay in the stud and the head will pull through the trim. If necessary gouge the plaster to get your pry bar under the trim so you won't mark the wood.

This is a good time to send the woodwork out for dip strip-ping if a wood finish is feasible. Wood that has lost its detail under many layers of paint should be stripped even though it will be repainted.

Remove plaster castings on the ceiling by cutting the plaster wall around them with a chisel and prying them down along with the plaster under them. A saber saw worked at a tilt does a good job of cutting the medallions loose.

Leave the kickboard in place. It will end up recessed in the new wall one-half inch but the pot belly molding will hide the discrepancy. With nails at top and bottom, kickboard is almost impossible to remove without splitting. But if you must remove it, pry the top out evenly along the length of the piece. Insert the pry bar as deeply as it will go and place a scrap of wood behind it to act as a fulcrum.

If you leave the window and door trim in place and butt the wallboard against it, it will be recessed in relation to the new wall and won't look right. And it has no trim to hide the change in depth.

If you do remove the window and door trim, it will be raised ½ inch from the frame when you replace it over the new wall.

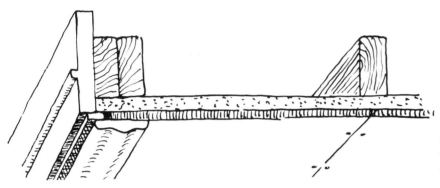

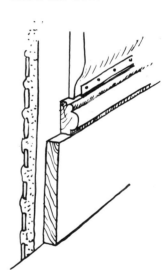

If you apply new wallboard over the old plaster, a ½-inch strip of wood will be needed under the trim.

Fill this gap with a ½ by 1 inch strip of wood. Step the filler strip midway between the frame and the trim to avoid producing a long crack between pieces of wood.

While the window trim is off the sash weights of double-hung windows will be exposed. This is a good time to replace the weight cords. (Instructions can be found on page 57).

If you cannot remove the pot-belly molding on top of the kickplate, the wallboard can be butted against it although the finished wall will project over the molding that logically should go on top of it. Finish off the edge of the plasterboard with a special aluminum strip made for trimming plasterboard. An aluminum corner bead, which you should have on hand for outside corners anyway, can be used if you cut down one side of the strip with a pair of tin snips. It is difficult to produce a straight edge with wallboard compound if you have no ridge to guide the broadknife.

Removing the plaster from the lath will save removing the trim and moldings. Plaster castings, chair rails and picture-hanging strips have to be removed before the plaster comes down. One-half-inch plasterboard is about the same thickness as plaster. Some shimming may be needed to match the new and the old if the plasterboard butts up against plaster. Almost any discrepancy in level can be feathered out so it can't be seen if you spend the time on it.

Cut the plaster along the woodwork by scraping it with a chisel or very stiff knife. The plaster should be left under the woodwork with plasterboard butted up against it. The plasterboard can be inserted under the wood slightly but the long tapered edge shouldn't be used or it will produce an unnecessary extra taping job. Shim if necessary so that no gap is left between the plasterboard and the woodwork.

Use cut-down corner bead to provide a ridge for filling the bevel.

Walls were cut down to increase the light in this attic. The cut-down walls will get a wooden cap to finish them off.

Plaster cornices or large lath and plaster coves are best left in place at the top of the wall and repaired if necessary with plasterboard compound. If you remove the plaster from the wall and ceiling, saw above and below the cove with a circular saw set just deep enough to cut the plaster but not the lath to assure that the cove is not disturbed.

If you are doing more than one room, rent a Dumpster and build a chute to carry debris out of the house. Dumpsters rent for about $60 a month in most urban areas. The garbage company will deliver and pick them up. A chute made of plywood or corrugated tin roofing will greatly reduce your debris problem: you simply toss everything out the window.

When all the wallboard is nailed in position, tape the seams. The long sides of the wallboard are beveled so there is room for the taping job without raising the level of the wall. The short edge and the cuts you make will not have this bevel and the taping job will rise above the surface a bit. As the joint is feathered over 12 inches or so, this slight build-up is not visible. If there is any rough paper rising up from your cut, rub it down smooth with the handle of the razor knife.

Lay a coat of taping compound over the seam and immediately line the seam with perf tape. (Perf tape is paper with perforations to allow the taping compound above and below it to meld.) The paper adds fiber to prevent flaking of the compound when it's dry.

Push the perf tape flat with a broadknife, using a scraping motion in both directions to get most of the mud from beneath the tape. Don't scrape out so much that the tape comes loose; you want it to be bedded in mud but as close to the wallboard as possible.

Immediately recoat the seam with mud, using your broadest knife resting on the wall so the second coat is scraped smooth and flat.

Fiberglass woven tape sticks directly to the wall and cuts the first mudding down to one operation but is thicker than perf tape and shouldn't be used on seams that don't sit in a depression. Use it on the long tapered seams, if you're industrious enough to keep both types of tape on hand.

Give the nail depressions a coat, using the wood-backed broadknife as a mud carrier and scraping your working knife clean between strokes. From this point forward, use two knives, continually scraping the working knife clean on the other. Coat the nail dimples each time you coat the seams.

The first coat of mud will dry overnight in most climates. Subsequent coats should be much thinner and will dry in less time. The first coat can be made to set faster by mixing 1 part Fixall or Durabond 90 with 1 part wallboard compound. This hybrid mud won't set as fast as straight Fixall but will harden fast enough to allow the first finish coat to go on the first day.

Inside corners require a special corner knife for a professional-looking job. The knife blade is bent at ninety degrees for spreading mud over perf tape and it costs about $8. Fold the perf tape before setting it into the corner. You can make inside corners without using the corner knife by smoothing down the mud with your finger at the very corner and using a broadknife on the two walls. The final passes must be on the straight walls and will leave ridges in the corner on both sides of the angle. Take this down with sandpaper.

Inside corners less than 90 degrees must be done by fingers, broadknife and sandpaper.

Outside corners can be taped like any other seam but are a lot faster with an aluminum corner bead. Cut the bead to length with tin snips and nail it over the plasterboard. As the aluminum is not very strong, it should be laid over a heavy coat of mud. Pound the nail until it sits just flush with the metal. Don't make an indention. The bead sticks up enough to provide a ridge for the broadknife to ride on above the nailheads.

Give the seams a quick sanding to remove crumbs of mud. If

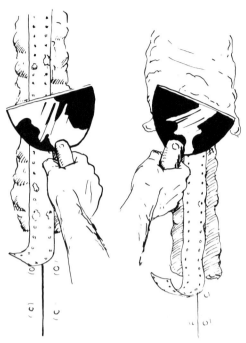

Perf tape covers the seams in the new wallboard

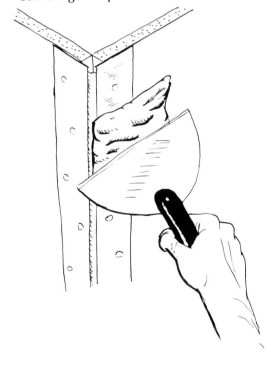

Corners get a special bead.

Putty Knife

you've been careful not to allow any large buildups, this sanding will go very quickly. One or two passes will knock off irregularities. If a larger buildup of mud should dry before you notice it, take it down with a jack plane or a paint scraper before sanding. Chip it off if you have to. Depressions can be filled rapidly and high spots look terrible.

Recoat the seams and nail-dimples. Any place that will hang onto mud through a thorough scraping needed it. Figure on four or five coats before you have all the seams and nailings completely smooth on your first job. A pro can do the job in two coats. You may never hit professional speed but you will get professional results on your first effort if you keep at it.

Seal the wall with primer before painting to prevent the lime in the plaster from burning through and also to point up flaws in the finish coat of mud. When using white self-priming paint, splash wall-sizing (a $1 powder that you mix with water) on the seams and nail dimples to be sure the lime stays down. Clean and paint the molding before replacing it. Seams that are painted can be filled with Spackle after the trim is up.

Fancy plasterwork is restored by adding plaster with a broadknife or paintbrush and scraping it away with a scraper, nailfile, soupspoon, sandpaper or whatever fits. Sometimes a construction made of wood or other materials is the answer. Anything painted with plaster should be glued in place with mastic so that it can't move the least bit. One coat of sealer and one coat of sizing will produce a surface that will hold plaster. Use perf tape wherever you can.

Victorians sometimes put dowels in the corners of special walls like the one around the chimney and fireplace. One inch dowel with a one-quarter segment ripped out on a table saw is nailed to the corner stud. The plaster wall stops short of the dowel with the crack between them filled with plaster so that the dowel produces a round inside a depression. Near the floor or near trim that requires a 90 degree corner, the plaster continues over the dowel to make a square.

Molding applied directly to the wall and painted with the same paint should be glued in place with panel adhesive so that no crack shows between it and the wall. If the wall is uneven, Spackle any cracks under the wood. The effect is colonial and requires a very formal room. Glue plaster castings in place with panel adhesive which is thick enough to fill uneven surfaces.

Concave walls can be covered with wallboard by slitting the back of the board every 4 inches with a razor knife. Starting at one end, nail the wallboard frequently enough to cause every slit to snap so the wallboard lies flat to the wall everywhere. With a flexible 6-inch broadknife fill every other joint with the least possible amount of mud. Push the broadknife hard into the wall to produce the round shape. When this is dry, fill the intervening series of joints. Sand and feather.

Convex surfaces are handled in the same manner except that the wallboard is slit on the front surface and the joints are taped.

If it is possible to save the old lath and plaster round wall with Fixall and mud, smoother shapes usually result. If you apply wallboard over the old plaster, dress the edge of the plasterboard with an aluminum edge and allow the change in level to attract interest to the curve.

Alternatives to wallpaper are mostly cheap but require some artistic skill. Block prints are easy and produce fairly accurate detail with random small missing patches. Thick latex paint works the best because it makes a good seal between the block and the wall. Cut the block out of anything soft that will stand up to water; beaverboard and acoustical ceiling tile cut easily with an Exacto razor knife and will make about forty good prints before getting soggy. A potato will work too.

Repeat patterns can be used to make a frieze where Victorians would have used wallpaper to emphasize and expand the cornice molding at the top of the wall. Often the ceiling was also decorated for the same reasons.

Where heavy traffic or frequent wiping might dirty a wall (as along the top of the chair rail or the handrail in a staircase or behind the splashboard on a kitchen or bathroom counter),

Wood Backed Taping Knife

Stairwells and halls get a lot of traffic and will need wall work in an old house. In this case some steps and the plasterboard both needed replacement.

the pattern can be varnished or sealed with clear plastic resin to provide a good surface to wipe. The same sealer without a pattern would call attention to itself by its shininess.

Stencils make a cleaner print. Make your own or order Megan Parry's from the catalog in the back of this book.

Graining rollers and grain combs were used at the turn of the century to reproduce the look of marble or wood on painted surfaces. Wallpaper-like patterns, unchanged since the Depression, are available (along with combs and rollers) from Darien Products.

The other way to go is texturing. If the wall is patched and finished but still has an irregular finish, you can texture it with joint cement left over from taping seams.

A stipple finish is anachronistic for a restored Victorian but is in keeping for most houses built between the wars.

Use a heavy-duty carpet roller. (Buy the $4 roller; the lighter one will disintegrate at the cardboard core.) Roll joint cement on the wall as it comes from the bucket, feathering each new pass into the prior one. The mud will adhere to both the wall and the roller, breaking loose in sharp strings. The suction between the roller and the wall is enough to pull loose rotten plaster so the wall *must* be sound. The moisture will loosen wallpaper causing sags. You can use mud to remove stubborn wallpaper, but don't try to stipple over it.

As soon as the whole wall is covered with stipple, smooth down the sharp ridges with a broadknife, cleaning the knife on a second knife after each pass. The result is an attractive textured surface.

Both the rolling and smoothing operations can be done on the end of a stick to increase your reach. Even for areas within reach a stick is a help because the laden roller is heavy and the stick adds leverage. If you don't have a commercial extension, tape the roller and broadknife to a broomhandle. The last inch

Taping compound, used straight from the can, can be used to texture a wall.

of wall all around is left plain, which looks fine. Remove any mud that splatters onto the ceiling or kickplate before it dries.

The dry stippled wall should be painted with wall-sizing, which will prevent the lime in the mud from ruining your paint job.

The stippled wall may be sanded lightly and painted with oil- or water-based enamel. A second coat, a shade darker can be painted on and immediately rubbed off, giving you an excellent two-tone wall.

Refinishing wood floors is the cheapest treatment for any area larger than about 10 by 12 feet, the size of the cheap carpet remnants. Any area up to about 30×40 can be refinished in three days for under $100, a total you'll appreciate if you price carpet or even vinyl tile. Wood looks good even with flaws and patches and is easy to maintain with the new plastic finishes.

A heavy-duty belt sander and special edger rent together for about $10-15 a day. If you rent the machinery around noon, you'll have time for the final sanding the following morning and can get the machinery back within 24 hours. Sandpaper will cost you another $25 for two good-sized rooms. Overbuy in all three grades and return what you don't use. It's senseless to risk a delay in the project because of running shy of paper and it's catastrophic if you cut back on the sanding.

After removing the furniture, seal off the work area as well as possible to keep the dust and then the fumes from the drying finish from attacking the whole house.

Remove the quarter round from the kickboard all around the room so that you can sand all the way to the wall. Doing this may seem unnecessary but it will guarantee you a perfectly straight edge where the floor meets the wall. The best way to remove quarter round is to find each nail by looking and then pound it through the kickboard with a punch. Where old nails are frozen in position, two screwdrivers can be used to pry the quarter round loose but be careful to use a pad or block of wood to avoid gouging the kickplate or floor.

You are ready to sand. The first grade of paper is extremely coarse, 25 grits per square inch, and is used only to remove the old finish and the deep gouges. Start with the belt sander and do half the room, running with the grain at all times. Any deep cross-grained scratches you put in the wood will be very difficult to remove with finer grades of paper. Always start the machine while the paper drum is off the floor and slowly lower it to contact, beginning to move back and forth immediately when it touches. As soon as you have done half the room (this probably won't take longer than 10 minutes) turn around and do the second half, carefully overlapping the first area sanded. At the end of each swing, lift the sanding drum off the floor, lowering it again as you begin the next stroke. Gouges and discolorations should be removed at this time as the finer grades of paper do a very poor job of digging. If you have a lot of gouges, you might consider leaving them. Floors are antiques too.

During this stage of the sanding and the two that follow, keep a hammer and nailset handy. Nails will be easy to spot with their shiny, newly polished heads. Set these ⅛ inch into the floor as you find them. Also nail any loose boards that show up. Avoid an inspection job later when you are tired. It's also a good idea to pick up any loose putty between the boards as it shows up.

When all the open area has been coarsely sanded, a rim about 4-inches wide will lay along each of the walls. This is removed by the edger, an industrial grade circular sander that can get right to the wall. The edger leaves crescent shaped scratches in the floor. Feather these out as well as you can and keep the edger moving at all times. With a much smaller surface working the floor, an edger will sink more easily into the wood than a belt sander. Some crescent scratches must be left to be removed in later sandings.

As soon as you have finished edging with the coarsest paper, restock the edger with medium-grade (40-60 grit) and re-edge. You'll be gratified to see the scratches left by the coarse paper disappear and you'll get the first look at your clean new floor. As the edger is a disk sander, the grit of the paper runs with the grain of the wood only on part of its rotation. Sanding second with the belt-sander will take out most of the cross-grain scratches. The large belt sander is always used second (except on the initial sanding).

Sand the middle of the room with the belt sander and re-inspect for nails to set and loose putty between the boards. Sweep up and save the sanding dust from this operation to make new wood putty (directions below).

If the floor is softwood and has been refinished before, you may notice high spots in the corners. Take these out carefully with a chisel and sand by hand.

Vacuum the room, taking special care to get any cracks between the boards clean. If you are going to stain the floors, do so now according to the instructions on the can. Areas that have been puttied will take less stain and appear light so you must stain before you putty.

Putty the nailholes and cracks between the boards with a mixture of glue and sawdust retrieved from the second sanding operation. This sawdust is free of finish yet isn't so fine that it's difficult to work. The mixture of sawdust and glue should approximate pancake syrup in consistency. Smear it across the newly sanded floor with a large broadknife, working it into the wood and scraping off the excess. As the mix becomes dry, scrape it off the knife into a second container and thin it with more glue. You'll be able to putty about 100 square feet in 15 minutes. By this time dinner is long overdue and you can knock off for the day.

The next morning your puttying job will be dry. Sand it with medium paper lightly to remove the roughness of the putty, starting with the edger and finishing with the belt sander. This operation will not take long as the putty sands easily.

Re-sand the floor with fine paper, starting with the edger and finishing with the belt sander. If you rented the sanding equipment at noon on the day before, you can now return it, just within the 24-hour time limit. Vacuum the room, being careful to catch any dust lurking on shelves and windowsills. Restain as needed.

The first coat of finish to go on the floor is sealer. This product is similar to the final finish but contains a fine filler ingredient which will fill in the pores in the wood and give a more lustrous final product. Be sure to shake the can until the filler is milky white.

Most of the new plastic finishes are painted on, allowed to seep and then wiped off, removing the problems caused by brush strokes or foreign matter. Follow the directions on the can.

Wait four hours for the first filler coat to dry and sand by hand to remove the fine wood fibers which will have stood to attention with the drying of this first coat of resin. This sanding sounds worse than it is as the fibers stand up individually and sand off very easily. No more than 15 minutes work with a piece of 100-grit sandpaper on a block will be necessary per 100 square feet of floor.

As soon as you are done sanding, wipe the floor with a slightly damp rag to remove the dust. As you are now homing in on your final product, dust becomes critical at this point.

Give the floor a second coat of filler, wipe away the excess and allow it to dry overnight. At the end of your second day, the floor is protected from discoloration and must be only kept free of dust.

The following morning, re-sand the floor by hand, wipe free of dust and apply your first coat of finish. This coat is applied like the filler, wiped away and allowed to dry for four hours. It must be hand-sanded and wiped again.

On the evening of the third day, you can apply your final coat of finish, wiping away the excess as in the earlier steps. If any dust settles into this coat, sand lightly when dry and touch up with a rag lightly dampened with finish. Replace your quarter round, using new round wherever necessary. This is one of the few jobs that can actually be done within the tolerances of a $1.98 wooden miter box. Paint the quarter round before you replace it.

Although hardware store products will do the job, special plastic resin glue, filler and finish should be purchased from a specialty floor shop.

WOODWORK: DOING YOUR OWN CARPENTER GOTHIC

Even if your intention is to produce a thoroughly modern job without a glance at anything in the past, the quality of your work will still be judged by the joints in your woodwork. You can improve the job greatly by utilizing some of the techniques developed by the Victorians who were masters of joinery. If

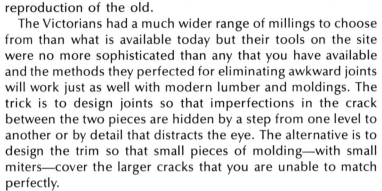

the new work is in eyesight of the older work, a little thought and a bit of molding will often serve to make the styles work together without making the new seem merely a bad reproduction of the old.

The Victorians had a much wider range of millings to choose from than what is available today but their tools on the site were no more sophisticated than any that you have available and the methods they perfected for eliminating awkward joints will work just as well with modern lumber and moldings. The trick is to design joints so that imperfections in the crack between the two pieces are hidden by a step from one level to another or by detail that distracts the eye. The alternative is to design the trim so that small pieces of molding—with small miters—cover the larger cracks that you are unable to match perfectly.

By the time you have determined the shape of your project and hidden all the joints in steps or under molding, your design will be finished.

Because you can't rip an edge straight enough to show with hand tools or mill rough-cut edges well enough with a jack plane to accept trim, your trim design will be limited by what lumber you can buy ready to cut to length. Lumber is available off the rack in 1/4-, 1/2-, 3/4-, 1-1/16-, and 1-3/4-inch thickness, but not all widths are available in all thicknesses. As most of your trim work will be done in 1-inch stock (which measures ¾ inch as you buy it); ¾ inch will be your standard trim increment. One-half- or one-quarter-inch stock can be used for inserts; 5/4 where you need a heavier appearance.

Sawing wood in the direction of the grain to make a board narrower is called *ripping* and is usually done with a circular saw although it can be done with a handsaw. Use an 8-point saw (8 teeth per inch) and keep the saw low enough to be guided by the kerf it has already cut but not so low that it chews up the wood before it gets serious about cutting it. Freehand rips should be faced to the back or otherwise hidden. Use factory edges where you will want to apply trim.

You can clean up a rip with a jack plane and round its edges with sandpaper to produce a good match with factory-milled edges that won't be trimmed.

Teflon-coated, small-toothed blades make a finer rip in plywood with a circular saw than with a combination blade although the ripping is slower. Set the blade to project ¼ inch through the plywood. If both sides of the rip are to show, clamp the plywood to a solid wood surface that will not damage the blade to minimize torn grain on the backside. Saw with the best surface up.

Small pieces of stock that are difficult to hold in place with your knee should be nailed to a work surface so they won't move while they are being sawn.

Sawing a board across grain to make it shorter is called "cutting." Most cuts are improved with a quick sanding to remove the last hairs of grain but the cut can't be altered with sandpaper or a rasp to improve a poorly fitting miter, which is why a good miter box is so important. Cuts are rarely made with a circular saw in trimstock unless the ends will be covered. A 10-point handsaw should be used for cutting.

Corners of rooms are never perfectly square because of the slight buildup necessary to taping the joint. Wood that is cut for a corner will fit better if you plane the last 3 inches of the backside with a jack plane. The final ¼ inch will usually require rounding with sandpaper to fit snugly against the plasterboard.

When cutting two boards to butt together end-to-end, saw them both at 45° and overlap them. The joint will sit down tightly enough to practically disappear. If putty is required, it will hold better than in a deep straight crack. Choose boards with similar color and grain to help hide the splice.

Dadoes require time and care but turn out well with hand tools. A miter box does the neatest job on trim stock. A circular saw can be used on plywood or particle board.

A quarter inch is adequate depth for dadoes to hold shelves in cabinets. Use a plywood blade and make test cuts, adjusting the depth until it's right. As the depth of the dado will determine the width of the cabinet, accuracy is important.

Cut the two sides of the dado carefully to make a snug fit for the shelf that will sit in it. Two quick passes between the cuts will prepare the dado to be cleaned up quickly with a chisel. A screwdriver will do a good job of knocking down the wood left standing between the cuts if you don't have a chisel handy.

A straight board can be clamped or tacked to the plywood or particle board as a ripping fence to guide the circular saw. Such a fence isn't adequate to guide a saw ripping ¾-inch plywood because the saw's tendency to wander is so strong it will either move the board or move away from it. But the fence will work well for the shallow cuts required here.

Glue the shelf with white glue and pull it tight into the dado with pipe clamps. Screws will do a good job of pulling the shelf into the dado. Often taps with a hammer will do the job.

If the fit is tight, round the edges of the shelf—not the dado—with sandpaper, or plane the shelf with a jack plane underneath. If the fit is loose, take up the slack with shavings taken from a piece of scrap with a pocketknife. Glue them into the dado underneath the shelf (or above it on high shelves where the bottom shows more) and trim the excess with a pocketknife after the glue has dried. If the job is sloppy, trim it with cove molding and call the molding an aid in wiping out the shelves.

Use a miter box to cut dadoes for medicine cabinets or shallow bookshelves, and lift out the scrapwood very neatly in the front of the dado if the unit will have no façade to cover the

Butt joints set at 45° will show less of a crack.

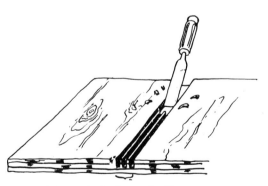

Making a dado for a shelf.

In this room using space economically was a necessity but the builder didn't want to darken the room by closing everything off with cupboards. The shelf under the stairs is supported with dowels, leaving the open feeling of light and air and also providing a good place to put the stereo.

end of the dado. A few extra passes with the backsaw after it has come to the bottom of its depth setting will assure that the dado is cut evenly along its length.

As soon as the cabinet is assembled, tack a diagonal piece of scrap somewhere in the back to keep the unit from being knocked out of line. Cabinets are fragile until they are hung.

Dowels make excellent shelf supports if the shelf isn't required to make the cabinet rigid. They are much cheaper than patented shelf hardware and are better looking. Dowels come in a variety of diameters, usually in 3-foot lengths. Wrap them in masking tape before cutting them to length, to minimize splitting, and round the lead edge with sandpaper before setting them. A series of holes down the side of the shelf unit will make adjustable shelves. A hand-held power drill will do the job accurately enough without a dowel jig. Pliars are usually required to remove the dowels and sometimes chew up their ends but as adjustable shelves are rarely actually adjusted, this isn't a real problem. Cut a few extra pegs while you are at it and tape them to the back of a shelf out of the way for later use.

Short shelves which will sit on dowels are best made of particle board or plywood because short lumber tends to warp just enough to sit badly. Shelves longer than three feet can be made of lumber if there will be enough weight on them to hold them down.

Adjustable shelves must be treated the same on top and bottom to control warpage. If the top gets formica, formica the bottom also; the same with finishes. This is unnecessary with fixed shelves unless they span great distances.

Dowels are sometimes used on fixed joints to take the place of screws, especially in furniture. A dowel will give as the piece flexes where a screw will tend to chew up the wood around it. Dowels to be used in this manner can't be cut from long dowel stock because it isn't milled with enough accuracy. Special pre-cut and pre-grooved dowels must be used. The groove carries glue with it into the joint. Usually a dowel jig is used for high tolerance work. These sell for about $10 and will guide the drill for twenty or thirty holes before they get too sloppy for the type of accuracy required.

Pre-cut, pre-grooved dowels can be cut down and used as plugs to cover screw heads. These must be allowed to project in the finished job because the end grain is difficult to work flush without eating away at the wood around it. If you want to cover screw heads and work the job flush afterwards, (as on a counter or tabletop) get a plug-cutter made for the job. The grain on the cut plug runs in the same direction as that on the countertop and will sand flush.

Dowels are produced by shaper heads, as is molding, so diameter isn't always standard. If you want to use heavy dowels for pegs as in a staircase, shop around until you find a dowel that matches a hole you are able to drill.

Cutting, ripping and dadoing are the primary carpentry steps available to you. The rest of the plan is a matter of designing your way out of joints that you won't be able to pull off.

Any wood joint longer than an inch is a likely cause of problems if the design calls for the two pieces to sit flush with an indistinguishable crack between them. This sort of furniture-grade joinery requires careful jigs and clamping during the gluing process. Room trim, which isn't glued and which is mounted to irregular walls, can't be joined with such accuracy.

Doors are framed with more precision than any other part of the house because their function depends on it. Even here, where the 90° corners are accurate, a mitered or butted joint between the upright jamb and the horizontal crown will fall short of the sort of perfection called for in a flush-trim job. The slightest variation in the wall or in the match between the wall and the door frame will be carried to the top corner joints where it will show. Even if the lineup is perfect, shrinkage of the wood over time will sabotage the joint.

Modern designers simply accept the bad joint as one of the characteristics of functional design. The Victorians added a

The molding separating the upright jambs from the crown of this door frame is functional —the rest of the design is exuberance.

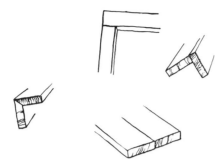

These joints will open.

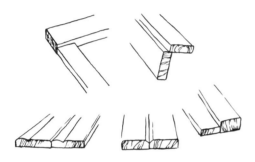

These joints won't show it.

step to the joint—a strip of wood along the bottom of the crown serving to emphasize the crown and give it heft—and eliminated the need for the jamb and crown to line up perfectly.

The step may be as simple as a strip of parting bead or any molding which projects beyond the level of the jamb and crown. Bull-nose stop is manufactured with one rounded edge for use as a parting bead to separate double-hung windows, and is still widely available. It has a simple rounded edge on one side and the two ends can be quickly shaped with sandpaper to produce matching rounds. If a more elaborate milling is used to provide the step, it should be mitered so that the detail in front carries around the edge to the wall.

Step joints were also commonly produced by making one piece thicker than the ones that butt into it. A very simple trim design would butt 1-by-6 jambs into a 5/4-by-6 or 5/4-by-8 crown. One-by-four is often used to trim doors as a means of saving money. Unfortunately, the jambs look like they were chosen to save money. A piece of frame molding made for the job and sold at lumber dealers or chosen from a frame shop adds grace to the crown of a door, although it's not needed in solving trim problems.

Victorians often used a heavier piece of wood at the bottom of door jambs to suggest a plinth at the bottom of a classic column and to help hide the match between the jamb and the kickplate that runs along the floor. This technique is especially useful if the pieces to be matched are elaborately milled or if one component (the pot-belly molding on top of the kickplate in this case) would project illogically. Elaborate fluted trimstock is very expensive but 5/4 will add the effect of a plinth to a new job and solve the bad miter where the kickplate meets the door jamb.

Thicker stock was also sometimes used at the top corners of doors and windows when the same milling was used to traverse both the top of the opening and the sides. In this case the raised corner was usually square and usually decorated to justify its presence. The corner block might be milled with round decorations, called a bullet, or festooned with decorations of gesso, pressed wood or real wood carvings. Bullets are still difficult to find, but pressed wood appliques are widely sold in large hardware stores.

Stepped joints can also be used between boards that lay parallel where the step distracts the eye from the long crack. Some lumber, meant to be used as paneling, is milled with a bead which hides the crack. You can manufacture your own by putting a small bevel on the edge of both boards before mounting them.

Long joints are more often hidden with moldings. The two most widely available are quarter round, which is a quarter of a circle in profile, and cove molding, which has a quarter circle milled out of it with a lip left on the two edges. Both are available from ¼ inch and up in size. The two flat backsides are of different sizes so that you can turn the piece to avoid having the edge of the molding come flush with the edge of the board and producing a new long crack to take the place of the one you are hiding.

Where the board meets a wall as along the top of a kickplate, a pot-belly molding is a better choice than either quarter round or cove molding. The pot-belly molding is designed to pull tight to the wall without providing a straight line atop the kickplate which would show how crooked the wall is. Sources of hard-to-find moldings, including several pot-bellied ones, are given in the back of this book.

Picture-frame shops often have the widest selection and best prices on stock that can be used as moldings. The smallest and simplest frame is elaborate by molding standards and what the framer considers the bottom of his line is sometimes much cheaper than what the lumberman considers the top of his.

Moldings which touch the wall should be nailed sparingly so they can be removed when it comes time to paint. Moldings which hide the crack between cabinets and the wall should be nailed to the wall rather than to the cabinet. The crack will show less.

Cabinet corners are more of a problem because the trim detail designed to finish off the edges of boards to form the façade of the cabinet must be carried consistently around the larger open surface of the side. This usually involves a two-level side, with the plywood cabinet wall forming a lower plane and trim forming a higher, with molding framing the joints. Larger surfaces might be divided by an additional piece of trimstock to break the lower surface into smaller units. This additional division is usually set vertically to give the appearance of bearing weight.

The Victorian theory of proportion suggested that cabinets duplicate classic buildings on a small scale with the surface broken into three vertical divisions. This would suggest a wider trimstock at the top to give added emphasis even though this means a shorter door and reduced access to the top shelf of the cabinet. The top "third" was often separated from the rest of the cabinet by a molding which serves to hide the necessary long joint between the horizontal and vertical trim (as bull-nose stop does to the trim on a doorway). Detailing was added most lavishly to the top section, then to the bottom, finally to the middle to avoid what was felt to be an unfinished look. If very little detailing was used, it would be added first to the top part, then on the bottom, and only lastly would any be added to the middle.

Two levels can also be used to decorate drawer fronts and cabinet doors, and provide a place to hide joints.

The drawers in this carpenter Gothic china cabinet were decorated with a buildup of 1×1s and picture-frame molding. The extra decoration (now about 25¢ a foot including 1×1s and framing) provides enough distraction to hide the crack around the drawer which is usually unattractive in flush-set drawers.

If a picture-frame molding can be used and can lap over the edge of the level 1×1 and this edge can be ripped at home with a circular saw. The 1×1 with the rough-ripped edge goes in the

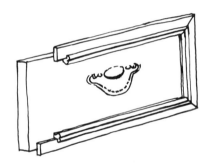

Picture-frame molding can be used to hide the crack where the drawer sits flush.

notch in the picture frame that was intended to carry the glass.

The outer frame of 1×1 can be reduced to ½-inch stock and set to lap beyond the edge of the drawer overlapping the cabinet façade to produce the dado used to keep drawer fronts from appearing unnecessarily heavy. A drawer stop is important in such a design to keep slamming of the drawer from working the trim loose.

Drawer fronts this heavily decorated require heavy decoration elsewhere on the cabinet for balance, especially on the crown. Simpler treatments for drawers and cabinet doors are suggested in the chapter on kitchens, where these are most often used.

Picture-frame molding was added to form a cap on the post in this entryway and help match it to the all-new pillar at the turn in the stairs. Stripping paint from the bannister, parson's bench and steps took a week. The finish is walnut-stained varnish dulled by steel wool.

The carpenter Gothic pillar is three pieces of 1×8 custom ripped with a circular saw and faced with ½-inch stock to produce insets and match the existing post. Strips measuring ½×1 were ripped at 45° to produce the corner of the pillar. The self-ripped miters proved too crude so the pieces were reversed and the bad crack was covered with half round.

Five pieces of ½-inch stock form the cap. Plywood under these holds them together so they can be nailed to the irregular ceiling as a unit. Molding covers the edge and hides the plywood. It's removable for painting.

Interior posts are usually hollow and are installed before the flooring goes in while the carpenters have access to the floor joists. Loose posts are best tightened with wedges and new lag bolts with washers set into the joists while the ceiling is open in the room below. If this is impractical, remove the kickplate, destroying it if necessary. A chisel may be required to remove some flooring around the kickplate. Keep this small enough to cover later with quarter round. When you have exposed the body of the pillar under the kickplate, drill or saber saw a 2-inch hole to provide access to the far side of the post. With a long bellhanger's bit and a socket set, you can add lag bolts and washers from the inside. A loose bannister can be tightened by removing the cap of the post and adding lag bolts from within.

The trim finishing off the floorboards on this landing is a single milling. It could be approximated with a large dowel flanked by picture-frame molding on ½-inch board. Stain, glue and putty the assembly before installing it to avoid a crack opening between components.

A 6×6 post and 3×12 beams stand in place of the original exterior walls in the house on the next page and bear the weight of the upper story. The roof is nailed to the top of 2×8 rafters, the plasterboard ceiling to the bottom. A 2×10 corner joist required by the building code projected through the ceiling and produced this design. The 1×2 flanking the corner joist makes the "beam" heavy enough to look right and covers the

This farmhouse was expanded with the 6x6 post and beams taking the place of the bearing walls.

edges of the plasterboard, simplifying the taping job. Tom Ward did this job for Lee and Jane Mizrahi of Sebastopol, California.

Plywood or particle board is too rough to wipe clean easily even after several coats of paint. Canoe-shaped patches in the veneer will show through. Spackle does a fine job of filling minute cracks and solving these problems. The best time to Spackle is after you have cut the plywood or particle board but before cutting dadoes. Coat any plywood that will be painted with primer designed to adhere to raw wood. Let it dry and sand quickly with 60- or 100-grit sandpaper, about two minutes to a surface. Use long strokes and a sanding block.

If you use a block of scrap wood for a sanding block, put a pad of folded paper towel between the block and the sandpaper. The pad will keep the sandpaper from wearing out so quickly and make it sand faster.

The pre-mixed canned product is more convenient for occasional jobs like this, although powdered Spackle is cheaper. Spread the compound with a broadknife, scraping away as much as possible as you go. Re-sand when it's dry. This quick step will give you a final paint job that won't show patches.

This knee-high work table can be knocked together easily and used for sawing plywood.

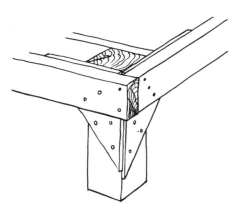

If you add plywood triangles at the legs you can make the table permanent.

For working plywood a kneehigh work table is a big improvement over saw horses. The dimensions aren't critical but height should allow you to comfortably rest your knees on the stock you are sawing. Frequent cross members will keep freshly cut plywood from binding the blade or falling to the floor and tearing up the last inch of the cut. If you make the table large enough, you can mount your miter box to it and still have room to work. Leave the 2×4s the length they come and you can use them later.

If you have a large enough shop area to keep the table, add plywood triangles to the legs to make it permanent. Without the triangles, the table will last long enough to do one kitchen.

A cheap rug from the Salvation Army will protect the floor of your work area and help control the mess. The foam-backed ones lay the flattest.

Plywood or particle board edges are ugly even after several coats of paint. You can finish off the edge in a variety of ways according to the tools you have available. The extra work before the cabinet is assembled will bring joy every time you open the door.

Give the shelf edge a coat of primer and Spackle as you do the flat surfaces. Two minutes of sanding will round the edges and hide the veneer.

A much more satisfactory method, however, is to face the shelves with wood. One-by-one will perfectly trim ¾-inch plywood or particle board without complicating the assembly of the cabinet. Finishing nails will do an adequate job of holding the 1×1 in place while the white glue dries. Drill holes before you nail to avoid splitting the trim and to keep the veneer in the plywood or the chips in particle board from throwing the nail out of line, carrying the trim with it. A small crack will show where the trim is applied but won't be large enough to gather dirt. At worst it will attract attention to the fact that you took the time to do a decent job.

Getting rid of the crack for a furniture-grade job isn't difficult but it does require additional tools. The trim piece must be clamped rather than nailed while the glue is drying so that the seam is nearly invisible. The trim piece must be slightly heavier than the shelf so that wood can be removed after gluing to make the fit perfectly flush. A pro would use a joiner for the job in the shop, or a router at the site. The manual that comes with the router will tell how to make the necessary jig.

You can smooth the facing with a belt sander after most of the excess wood has been taken down with a jack plane. A disk-sander, even with 100-grit sandpaper, is likely to leave waves which will look worse than would the crack, left alone. If you have access to a router, a jig for taking down edging is one of the handiest jigs you can build. A base of plywood large enough to hold the router with a guide screwed onto it will do the job. Adjust the depth of the cut by trial and error, using wing nuts to hold the router to the base and sliding it until the cut is perfect. Formica on the bottom of the base will make the unit slide more easily. Round the lead and trailing edges.

If the shelf facing is important but you don't have a router or belt sander, glue it yourself and pay for a couple of passes over a joiner at a cabinet shop. If the shelves are clean and ready to go, the cost will be only a couple dollars. If facing also goes down the two ends of the shelf, a router must be used. As set-up time is greater for this, the cost will be higher.

As you can't mill wood with hand tools, your projects will be determined by the materials you can find. Your dealer can be as important to you as a librarian

Choose a lumberyard nearby that will allow you to roam the stacks and do all your business there. Once the clerks get to know you they'll spend more time answering your questions. They'll be more likely to remember the oddball piece out-back that will do your job cut-rate. They'll deliver smaller quantities or special orders without making you wait two weeks. The large discount houses that handle lumber and materials can save you money, but they often hire clerks with no special knowledge of their field, and you give up a good source of free consultation when you use them.

If you do a carpentry job for someone else, mention it and ask for a 20 percent discount. If you are renovating your own house as an investment (you are), ask for your discount the first time you have an order that runs several hundred dollars. (As soon as you have enough feel for what you are doing to talk for three consistent minutes and sound like a pro, you'll get it.)

It's important to be able to wander through the stacks to see first hand what your dealer has that week. The lumber industry is probably the truest laissez-faire market in the country. Stock and prices change continually. An excess in a grade of 2×4s will drop the price of that grade dramatically or create a storefront pile of 49¢ specials. Twelve-cent-a-foot cove moldings will appear in a bin in random lengths for 15¢ apiece.

Products that you don't even know exist will stand there in racks and bins and suddenly change your thinking about a

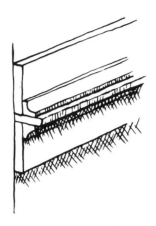

This facia is not only cheaper than a single clear board, but also less likely to warp or split with time.

project. Sometimes a flawed piece is graded into a low-price bracket although it's clear along the edge that matters to you. But you *must* be able to pick the individual piece yourself.

The best lumber is cut across the annular rings toward the bark of the log. Heartwood, which was once the growing tip of the tree, is usually filled with knots. Pin knots are no problem and often add interest. Knots larger than ½ by ¾ inch may shrink enough to fall out and are usually surrounded by grain swirls which can't be planed and are difficult to sand. Large knotted lumber is graded "common." It can be very rough, contain skips, and may even break at a knot. Better pieces are graded "standard and better" which is the standard framing-lumber grade. Knot-free lumber or pieces with small tight knots are graded "clear," which is the first acceptable trim grade. Some retailers select out vertical grain stock and sell it for extra money. Others will do so if you ask them to but there's a charge if you specify "VG" and you usually can pick the pieces yourself without having to pay extra.

Lumber shrinks in width but not in length as it dries. Most of the lumber sold is kiln-dried and the majority of the shrinkage has occurred before the lumber is planed and sold. Some shrinkage will continue to occur for several years. The shrinkage occurs along the annular rings and can cause a clear board sawn "open face" to curl. Lumber sawn across the annular rings to produce "vertical grain" is less likely to shrink and curl, and should therefore be used for cabinet trim or facia strips exposed to the weather.

Green or undried lumber is used most often for decking and for heavy beams where shrinkage in width won't cause a problem. Green select fir sells for about half the price of kiln-dried clear. Wait a month before applying stain or oil so the wood can dry. If the sun beats directly on the deck, apply the finish at the first sign of curling. If the bottom of the 1×4 decking is open to the air except the short stretch that sits on joists, curling will be minimal. Saw out large knots which may fall out as the wood shrinks.

For facia boards, green lumber wider than 4 inches is risky. Two pieces, with a detail to hide the crack between them, will be a lot less likely to curl.

When estimating lumber for a project, add up every piece in the plan and add 20 percent to make up for loss to scrap, errors and small design changes. For large projects such as kitchens or bathrooms, buy twice as much 1×2, 1×3 and 1×4 as you figure you'll need. These trim sizes get used in unbelievable quantities and if you do have some left over, you'll easily find a use for it.

Lumber is bought and sold in board feet, expressed as so many dollars per thousand. A board foot is 1 foot square by 1 inch thick. One board foot will make 3 lineal feet of 1×4, 6 lineal feet of 1×2, one lineal foot of 2×6 or 1½ lineal feet of 2×4.

Retail prices of surfaced lumber are usually quoted in lineal feet, which is the measurement you are interested in. If the piece is quoted in board feet, convert to lineal feet (L.F.) on the basis of cubic inches. Clear 2×4s at $345 a thousand would sell for 34.5¢ a board foot or 23¢ LF.

A 2×4 leaves the sawmill measuring a full 2 inches by 4 inches. It is then kiln-dried and planed to 1⅝ by 3⅝ inches or 1½ by 3½ inches. Lumber is delivered smaller than its nominal size because of loss in planing rather than because of lowered contemporary standards, although modern high-production milling does remove more wood than was lost before World War II. If you are matching new wood into old, you'll have to use some ingenuity. Dimensions under 6 inches are usually ½ inch under nominal; over 6 inches the loss in planing is ¾ inch.

Plywood and particle board do not undergo planing (although the better grades do get a sanding). They don't vary between nominal and actual delivered sizes. A ¾ sheet of plywood measures a full ¾ inches.

The variety of plywoods made is great, with solid core, particle-board core, core with gaps, or clear core used for special applications. Of major interest is whether the glue used is waterproof and the appearance of the outside veneers.

"A" face plywood can be finished natural with oil or varnish; "C" face may have small knots or splits and "boats" where the veneer has been patched with no matching of grain. "C" face will require Spackle and must be painted. "D" face is downright ugly but structurally sound. ACX—which has one good face, one not so good, and waterproof glue on the exterior—is the most versatile grade around the house.

Hardwood veneers run $10 a 4x8 panel (in the case of birch) more than fir-faced plywood and go up from there. Vertical-grain fir plywood which matches the fir trim is available but will probably have to be ordered. If your lumberyard doesn't want to order only one or two sheets of fancy plywood for you, make your ire known and go somewhere else. Even the pros don't often order more than a sheet or two of fancy plywood at a time.

Building stairs is one of the hardest carpentry jobs you will encounter. The structural work shows and the least variation from "true" will cause a wobble. And you can't just start at one end and play it by ear, as you can with most projects.

Two 2×6s make a step that's less likely to warp than one made of a single 2×12. Three 2×4s look rustic.

Cheaper grades of heavy lumber are cut near the heart of the log. If you can see more than a small segment of an annular ring at the end of the board, it is likely to curl and shouldn't be used for a stair tread. Nails won't prevent a two-by board from curling.

More formal 5/4×12 stair treads of short laminated pieces with a milled front edge are inexpensive and weather well. Inspect the treads for open-face grain which may rise up when it gets wet. The glues used to make composite treads will last in any conditions but the mills are sometimes sloppy about the woods they use.

Building a successful set of stairs requires some planning and thought. You will not be able to design them as you go.

Stair stringers are one of the few carpentry jobs that must be done perfectly—everything shows.

Steps which project beyond the stringers appear to float. If they float so much that they look Japanese, they may be an anachronism in a period setting.

The standard rise for steps is 7¼ inches. To get the total number of steps, divide the total rise by 7¼ and subtract 1 (the porch counts as one step). If the answer doesn't come out a whole number, choose the nearest whole number of steps and adjust the rise between them. Anywhere between 6½ and 8 inches will walk comfortably.

The alternative is to set the steps at 7¼ inches except the bottom which takes up the odd remainder. The bottom step is never at eye level and will show the discrepancy least.

If you can't measure the rise directly from the porch to the ground because of terrain, hold a level to the side of a stepladder or an upright board placed at the bottom of the intended stairs. Sight down the level until the bubble is centered and the level is aimed at the porch or deck. Mark the ladder or board and measure to the ground.

The exposed tread is usually 10 inches. If you use 2×12 or 5/4-by-12 inch treads, they will overlap by 1-1/4 inches. The lead edge of the bottom step will be 10 inches times the number of steps from the porch or deck.

The length of the 2×12 you must buy for the stringers is 12½ inches times the number of steps plus 6 inches. You need two stringers for steps up to 4 feet wide, three for wider.

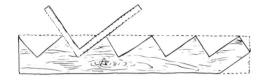

Mark a large framing square at 7¼ and 10 inches for standard rise stairs and lay the square on the stringer so the two marks are on the edge. The rise and tread will be lined up. Mark the cut out for the top step and move the square for the other steps down the stringer.

Cut the top of the stringer all the way through at the angle of the line for the 7¼ rise. Cut the bottom of the stringer parallel to the bottom step down 9 inches or so. The top and bottom cuts will equal 90°.

Place the stringer. The notch for the top step should sit 7¼ inches plus the thickness of the stair tread down from the deck. Resaw the bottom of the stringer to lower the top step.

When the stringer fits properly at deck and ground level, cut the notches for the treads. A circular saw cannot finish an inside angle. Finish the cut with a handsaw.

Hang the tops of the stringers with joist-hanging hardware or nail them to a 2×8 and nail that to the front joist of the porch. The top of the stringer may just catch the horizontal porch joist that it will be nailed to. Add to the bottom of the joist until you have a good nailing surface. When using 16 penny nails close to the end of a board, drill first to reduce risk of splitting.

A 2×8 on edge ties the bottom of the staircase together. This cross member should rest with the bottom of the stringers on concrete block or on a lower deck. A post for a handrail is bolted to the 2×8 cross member and to the stringer. The first or second tread is cut around the post.

If you cast a footing with metal straps bolted into the bottom

of the stringer, put strap on both sides and bolt through the wood so the fastening will remain solid when the stairs get old.

The stringers will last much longer if they are raised slightly from the concrete so they can't pick up moisture by osmosis. Water sealer should be used on all parts near the ground.

A more rustic set of stairs can be built with the treads resting on short blocks nailed to the inside of the stringers. The short blocks are the weak link in such a design because they can soak up water and decompose in a very few years. To lengthen their life insert each end in a can of water sealer for 2 to 3 minutes so the wood soaks up as much as possible. Pre-drill for nailing and splash sealer in the nail holes. Also treat the treads.

An upright 2×8 every 6 or 8 feet and at turns stabilizes the stringers. The treads alone are not adequate to hold the staircase together.

The stringer may be toe-nailed to the top of 4×4 posts but a notch makes a neater and stronger job. Carefully saw the outsides of the notch to match the stringer, then saw at random every ½ inch or so as for a dado. The notch will clean up quickly with a chisel or screwdriver and the stringer can be bolted through the post for a sturdier job. The post may continue up to support the handrail.

Concrete footings are available ready-cast to support the posts and keep them clear of the ground. Some are solid concrete with a dimple cast in the top. A lag bolt or heavy nail in the bottom of the post fits the dimple and keeps the post centered. Other footings have a wood top cast in place to which the post is nailed. Several thicknesses of roofing tarpaper, an asphalt shingle, or even an old 45 RPM record should separate the post from the concrete. Trim the moisture barrier to the edge of the post so it can't catch rain water.

As the ends of the treads and the short blocks don't have a good chance to dry out when they get wet, a naturally rot-resistant wood is a good choice. Cedar and redwood are the best species to use around constant moisture, but cedar is soft and will wear down rapidly with traffic, quickly making the stairs look like they have always been there.

A period *porch railing* is fairly easy to build with standard lumber store millings. Turned spindles with square ends to make the banisters are often available in plastic-wrapped hanging packages. These are expensive because so many are required. They can be alternated with much cheaper 2×2 or placed just at focal points and still produce an excellent effect. Banisters of 2×2 with no turned spindles also turn out well.

Handrail milled for stairwells and meant to be hung on metal supports work well above and below the banisters although clear 2×4 could be used, perhaps with a decorative bevel or routing. The handrail must be dadoed on a table saw. The banisters fit in the dado separated by short blocks of wood.

Buy your banisters or the 2×2 stock to make them before having the rails dadoed to be sure you get a precise fit. A loose dado makes the railing very difficult to assemble because friction will hold the unit together until it is tied or tacked in place to dry.

Apply stain and finish before assembly for a natural finish. Paint is also easier to apply before assembly but the last coat should go on after the unit is in place to cover glue joints, nail-holes and dings. New wood to be placed out of doors will require a coat of primer and two coats of enamel.

Cut the handrails to length before assembly while you can still get them in a miter box. Have the banisters and spacers cut to length with any ragged edges left from the cut sanded clean before mixing the glue. Waterproof brown glue stiffens in about half an hour so you must work rapidly once you've started. If the dado is loose, nail the spacers to the banisters before placing them in the dado.

Any spacers that slide out of line will be easy to spot. Tie these into position if necessary. Square the unit with a large framing square and wipe any glue that has squeezed out of the dado with a damp rag. If the glue has begun to set, a Teflon-pot scrubber will loosen it. Allow the unit to dry overnight before moving it.

The banisters and spacers must be cut at an angle for stairs. To get the angle use a carpenter's bevel which adjusts to measure odd angles, or hold a piece of scrap to the stair stringer, true it vertically with a level and mark it. Set the miter box to match the mark.

It is a good idea to try to assemble the railing on stairways to be sure the banisters are vertical and everything fits. After gluing, tack the unit in place to dry.

Two screws in each connect the handrail and bottom rail to the post. If the post is hollow, these may be set from inside. If 4×4 posts are used, screw the handrail to 1×3 and glue this to the post.

Nail one-by *decking* with 8 penny nails. Nail two-by decking with 10 penny nails. With either size decking, use a galvanized 16 penny nail to space the boards so that dirt will fall through the crack. A slimmer nail does not make a big enough gap.

Green select one-by lumber can be used for the deck. Cut out any knots over an inch in diameter that might fall out when the wood dries and shrinks. Allow the decking to dry a full month before staining unless the sun dries the top side so much faster than the bottom that the boards want to curl. Green two-by decking is riskier than one-by because drying takes longer and the top will shrink faster than the bottom.

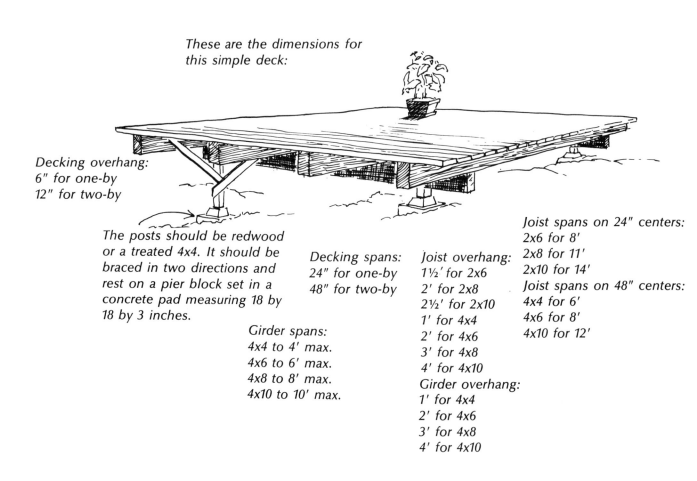

These are the dimensions for this simple deck:

Decking overhang:
6" for one-by
12" for two-by

The posts should be redwood or a treated 4x4. It should be braced in two directions and rest on a pier block set in a concrete pad measuring 18 by 18 by 3 inches.

Decking spans:
24" for one-by
48" for two-by

Girder spans:
4x4 to 4' max.
4x6 to 6' max.
4x8 to 8' max.
4x10 to 10' max.

Joist overhang:
1½' for 2x6
2' for 2x8
2½' for 2x10
1' for 4x4
2' for 4x6
3' for 4x8
4' for 4x10
Girder overhang:
1' for 4x4
2' for 4x6
3' for 4x8
4' for 4x10

Joist spans on 24" centers:
2x6 for 8'
2x8 for 11'
2x10 for 14'
Joist spans on 48" centers:
4x4 for 6'
4x6 for 8'
4x10 for 12'

Leave an inch gap where the decking meets a wall and the majority of the debris that gathers here will drop through.

Stagger the nails in the decking across the width of the board as you go from joist to joist so the board will not split.

A 4-by-4 post is adequate regardless of the size and weight of the deck. Cedar or redwood should be used for the post. If fir is used, soak the ends well in water sealer and provide a moisture barrier between the post and the concrete pier. (Concrete sweats.)

Precast pier blocks are available with wood cast in the top. Set the post on top of the pier and toenail it in place. Other blocks have a dimple in the top to accept a nail or lag bolt centered in the bottom of the post.

A pad of concrete under the block will protect it from the burrowing of rodents and erosion. One bag of ready-mix with sand and gravel in the same bag with the concrete is adequate per block. The post should be braced in both directions.

White glue (Elmer's is the best known brand) is squeezed directly from the plastic bottle and used on unfinished interior wood. Not good around water but adequate for kitchen cabinets. If enough water gets inside the cabinet to damage the glue joints, you have a problem that has to be fixed regardless of the glue you use. White glue dries milky clear and if it seeps out of cracks will prevent stain from absorbing into the wood. Wood should be clamped while gluing, though nails will hold solidly enough for non-structural trim.

Brown glue comes in powdered form and is mixed with water for use. It dries brittle-hard in a couple of hours, is too stiff to use a half hour after mixing. The mixing container should be disposable. Brown glue can be washed out of paint brushes if the job is completed before any glue sets up in the bristles. A cheap throw-away brush is usually the way to go. Clamped joints will dry stronger than the wood itself. Joints nailed while they are drying are usually adequate for cabinet work or outside trim. Use brown glue for exterior work or cabinetry around a shower or tub.

Contact cement is painted on both surfaces as it comes from the can. It's good for laying formica, mirrors or other sheet goods. Two coats are required on porous surfaces such as plywood. Both surfaces should be allowed to dry to the touch before being joined. Contact cement bonds instantly to itself so pieces must be perfectly aligned before touching. Clamping is unnecessary. It stays rubbery but is impermeable to moisture and should not be used for trim jobs where it might cause warpage.

Mastics are available in latex- or oil-based versions in quart or gallon cans or in 11-ounce cartridges for use in a caulking gun. Most of these are specialty products which you will need only when you wander into that project. The salesman will explain which one to use. Use mastic whenever you are gluing irregular surfaces where a thicker paste will help fill voids, such as mounting plaster ornaments to the wall, assembling complicated moldings (where you need the gaps filled), or laying flooring.

The high ceiling was given more heft in this tiny bath by a carpenter Gothic cornice of layers of 1x4, 1x2 and moldings. The bottom cove molding should have been nailed to the wall rather than to the cornice to hide the unevenness in the plaster.

WINDOWS, DOORS AND SKYLIGHTS: LETTING THE OUTSIDE IN

No improvement has ever been made on the double-hung window. The upper window opens to let hotter air escape from the upper part of the room while the lower window lets in the fresh air. So many double-hung windows don't work well anymore because they are so old. But they can be totally restored with less work and at less cost than they can be replaced with the cheapest and ugliest aluminum framed store bought windows.

Window shops and cabinet shops that do windows keep sash stock on hand for framing the glass. Cutting and placing four pieces for a new sash, the moving part of the window, is a simple job that a window shop does with jigs on hand. This is the sort of job where outside help is cheap. The rest of the window materials consist of inexpensive strips of wood—so there's little cost involved in building a whole new track. This is a job you can do yourself with a miter box.

If the window is unattractive, disassemble it and clean it up piece by piece. Two strips of wood run from top to bottom on either side forming the track for the lower sash. Remove these by inserting a wide chisel under them and prying. If you are careful to pry at each nail, you can remove these without damaging them. If a piece of wood must be gouged, make it the strips. You can replace them (although probably not with identical stock) for about 12¢ a foot. You don't want to damage the frame because you won't replace it and the damage will show.

The lower window will lift out toward you. Tilt it and remove the weight cords which lie in grooves in the sash. Tie a knot in these and stick a big nail through the knot so they can't fall back into the wall when you release them. Handling the window and cords is an awkward job for one person, so enlist a friend.

Remove the window. Have it reframed if the wood is rotten or if the paint shows chronic peeling on the lower parts. Loose paint or dark wood indicate that the wood is saturated with water. If the wood is dry and sound but suffers from twenty layers of paint, strip it.

Between the two sashes is a parting bead set in a dado in the outer window frame. This can be difficult to remove. If it is lightly nailed as it should be, pull it out of the dado with a pair of pliers. If it won't come, pound a chisel into it and twist until the grain splits. Half the piece will lift out. You'll be able to get a screwdriver under the other half at the break to pry it out. The parting bead is usually plain so replacing it with a perfect match to the original shouldn't be a problem.

Replace this strip with a 1/2×1-1/16 strip ripped out of a wider piece of ½-inch stock (the rough rip can be hidden in the dado), or use bull-nose stop which is readily available and made for the job.

With the parting bead removed on both sides, the upper window will come toward you. If it is painted in place, give it a series of raps with a hammer from the outside to break it loose. If light taps don't do the job, cut the paint with a pocketknife and use a pad of wood to protect the sash from hammer marks. Tie off the weight cords as you remove them from the sash.

If there is paint on the tracks for the sashes, it must be stripped with hand stripper. Refinish this with a clear finish that won't show wear. It can't be recoated later without filling the track and causing the window to stick so a pigmented paint is a poor choice.

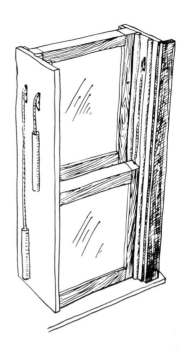

If the pulleys located in the upper end of the track have been painted or do not run smoothly, remove the screws and very carefully pry them out for stripping. New double-hung windows use a coil spring instead of counter weights and the sash-cord pulleys are hard to find. If you bend the stamped-tin frame, you will have to straighten it for reuse. Lubricate it with graphite; oil will gather dust and dry out.

Use special cord made for this job to replace sash cord. Woven cotten sash cord will not stretch or flatten as it crosses the pulley. No other cord will work as well.

A knot fitted in a slot fastens the cord to the window sash. Mark the frame at the height of this knot on the old cords so you know where it is when the window is closed. On some windows a door has been provided at the bottom of the outer frame. Remove the screw holding it in place and allow the weights to drop. Reach through the door and cut the old cord off the weights. Feed the new cord through the pulley and tie it to the weights.

Pull the cord until the bottom sash weight jams against the pulley. Back it off 2 or 3 inches and tie a knot at the level you have marked. The cord will be the right length to allow the window full run without the weight hitting the bottom.

To replace the cord on the upper window, allow the weight to strike the bottom of its well and pull up a full foot. Cut and tie the cord 4 to 6 inches below the pulley to match the groove in the upper sash. This weight raises as the window is opened. The weight for the lower sash falls.

If the outer window frame doesn't have a trap door, you have access to the weights through the wall trim. Remove the vertical jamb that sits flush on the wall on either side of the window. The weight well will be exposed.

Lubricate the window tracks with hand soap, wax or paraffin.

If the window is merely stuck due to swelling or paint, but otherwise in good condition, there are a number of things to try, all aimed at unsticking the sash from the tracks. A block of 2×4 on edge will sometimes spread the tracks a little and release the sash. The lower window can be lifted from outside. Don't pry by putting pressure on the horizontal wood. Pry on the two vertical side strips to avoid possible damage to the sash, moving from one side to the other. The upper sash usually rests in a track on both inside and outside so it's difficult to

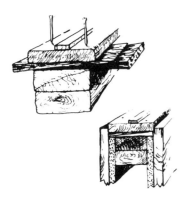

Insert 2-inch widths of cedar shakes from both sides until the door or window frame is aligned. Nail to secure the shakes and then saw off the excess.

pry. Remove the inside upper parting bead to get at it. Don't pound on the lower horizontal part of the sash or you'll tear the window apart. A sharp stiff knife can be used to cut the paint holding a window shut, though if the window has gone this far, you would do better to disassemble it and fix it properly.

Adding a new door or window to an old wall is the most satisfying sort of renovation job. The project ranges from heavy framing to fancy trim and entails the finest adjustments along the way. A circular saw with an old blade is needed to cut out the old wall. The rest of the job is done with hand tools. Cedar shakes are used as wedges to make the fit between the heavy studs and the door or window frame.

The job is simplest when one side of the wall is being replaced so you can completely open up the work area. This isn't necessary however.

Locate the studs on either side of where the new opening will be and cut away the interior wall. Finding studs isn't difficult: tap on the wall with your knuckles and listen for a solid sound; the space between studs will sound hollow. This will give you a close estimate of the location of the first stud to locate the approximate middle of the proposed opening. Drill a 1-inch hole and find the stud with your finger. From the center of this stud to the center of the studs on each side is sixteen inches. Studs are placed accurately on 16-inch centers on balloon-framed houses back to the 1880s.

Magnetic studfinders locate nails in the wall and cost about $3. These are used for hanging heavy pictures but aren't necessary if you're going to tear the wall open.

The wall must be cut to the inside edge of the stud on both sides of the new opening. If the opening is too wide, you can adjust it when you add the 2×4s that will hold up the header and fill in the extra wall you have cut away with wallboard.

If the wall is lath and plaster, nail every inch down the two studs that frame the opening to be sure that the lath is well nailed. A loose piece of lath will raise up when the sawblade hits it and tear loose plaster you don't want to lose. Set the nails just to the top plaster. If they are recessed at all, they will shatter the plaster and provide no grip where you need it.

Set your circular saw to cut about 1 inch deep up the vertical sides of the opening. Cut as deeply as possible across the top to cut into the studs, and do the same on the bottom if the opening is for a window. Use an old blade.

Before cutting the first side of the wall, make a short cut on each side and lift away a strip or two of lath or a 6-inch swath of wallboard to inspect for wiring or heating ducts. Moving wiring is simple; moving a heating duct is a major job. Vertical 2×4s nailed across the studs are firestops and can be taken out without harm to the wall, although they do add nails to the side of the stud and do your sawblade no good.

Cut the opening for a door 6 inches higher than the actual door to allow room for a 4×4 header and the frame. Cut the

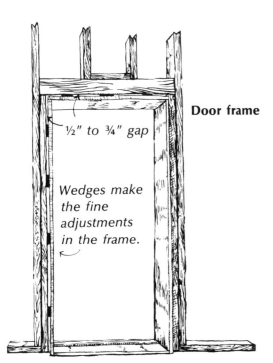

Door frame

½" to ¾" gap

Wedges make the fine adjustments in the frame.

opening for a window 6 inches higher and 6 inches lower than the sash. If the job is done neatly, you'll be able to cover the extra area cut away with trim. If you're not so lucky, some wall patching will be necessary.

The opening must be wide enough for the window or door frame with a 2×4 on each side to hold up the header, which supports any interrupted studs, plus allowing some leeway for adjustment.

When the first side of the wall is cut away, mark the four corners of the opening through the opposite side of the wall with a drill. The opening in the second side has to be large enough only for the frame to project. The extra width and height for studs and a header is needed only on one side.

Cut the siding on the second side of the wall away and finish off the interrupted studs with a handsaw. As the studs are accessible only from one side, you have an awkward sawing job of cutting them flush to the back of the siding.

Saw the soleplate that runs along the inside wall at both ends of the opening with a handsaw and pry it out. Unless the frame of the house is in bad condition you can cut two studs to make an opening 45 inches wide without concern for bearing walls. This is wide enough for nearly any door or double-hung window.

If you are cutting an opening for double French doors, a sliding glass door, or a picture window, check first to see if the wall you are cutting is supporting the house.

If the roof rafters or the floor joists for the second story rest on the wall you are cutting and more than two studs must be cut away, to give extra support to the ceiling joists in this way. Build a frame of 2×4s about 4 inches shorter than the height of the ceiling so it won't catch diagonally when you stand it up. Spread the weight across as much ceiling as possible to avoid damaging the plaster. A 1×12 or strip of ¾-inch plywood with a blanket on top will do. A 2×4 on the floor will take up most of the rest of the 4-inch margin. Cedar shingles tapped between the 2×4 on the floor and the support will take up the rest. Don't wedge the support so tightly that you damage the ceiling.

Set the support as close to the opening as you can and still have room to work. About 4 feet will do.

A 4×4 header is used at the top of openings up to 4 feet, a 4×6 up to 6 feet, a 4×8 up to 8 feet, and so forth. A 4×4 is adequate to support the sill of windows of any width. If you don't have a 4×4 handy, use two 2×4s upright with a ½-inch spacer between them so that both sides make contact with the two sides of the wall. If the original studs are unplaned and measure a full 4 inches, the new studs will need a ½-inch strip added to them to make them match.

Place the header with vertical 2×4s on either side to hold it up. Nail the new 2×4s to the old. If one of the new 2×4s must be lengthened to adjust the width of the opening, use scrap lumber or cut 2×4s to length to fill the gap and provide a nailing surface.

In this stud frame for a window opening the header should be:
4x4 to span up to 4 feet
4x6 to span up to 6 feet
4x8 to span up to 8 feet

The components for this window are all cut at 45° to make the octagonal shape. The glass is set as any picture window would be.

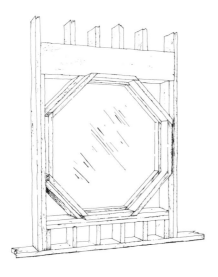

The interrupted studs may be irregular where you cut them off. Use cedar wedges to make a tight fit. Or lay a piece of 2×4 between them and nail to the studs and header. Drill nailholes before nailing this close to the end of a 2×4 to keep it from splitting, especially an old one, which will be very brittle.

Use a level to get the studs and header true.

The frame of the door or window is nailed to the studs and header with 2-inch-wide wedges of cedar shingle making the fine adjustment. Insert shingles on both sides until the frame is snug, drill so you don't split the cedar, and nail with finishing nails.

If possible, set the door or window in its frame for the final fitting. When the window operates smoothly and the door will stand open in any position without swinging open or shut, the frame is right. If it's not feasible to trial fit the door or window, use a large framing square.

Saw the excess cedar shake away but be careful not to chew up the edge of the frame that shows. Tap the bit of cedar left into the wall and cover it with trim to finish the job.

Salvaged double-hung windows come with the frame. Fixed-glass picture windows or homemade sliding windows should be framed with one-by stock. The frame is set flush with interior walls so the trim can be nailed to the wall and to the edge of the frame. It may be set flush and trimmed on exterior walls or project with the exterior siding butting into it.

Door-frame stock milled with a stop for the door makes a neater frame than a piece of one-by with a strip tacked on it. Set the door on two sawhorses and build the frame around it before setting it into the wall.

A heavy oak threshold milled for the job at about $2 a foot will do a professional finish job on doors leading to the outside. Thresholds aren't usually used on interior doors unless the flooring is chewed up during removal of the wall. If the flooring was done after the wall was built, it may be missing altogether. Fill the missing portion with one-by and floor patching compound to make a good base for the threshold. Bevel the edges of the one-by with a jack plane.

Prehung doors come ready to install with the frame, the door, hinges and sometimes even the latch and knob in place. The selection of doors is excellent with wood inserts and glass sections available but the hardware used is often so cheap that it will be out of place in an old house. Pay for better hinges and the custom work involved in placing them or place them yourself with a chisel. Tap the chisel in for the three sides of the recess you must make in the door and the frame for the hinge and then lift the wood out.

Two hinges should be used on interior doors—three on exterior.

You can Dutch any door that has a solid wood cross member at about the right height. It won't be as nice as a custom-made Dutch door, but if you have an old door on hand, it's almost free.

If the cross member is 8 inches or wider, you can get away with simply sawing the door in two. Clean the cut with sandpaper and apply top quality brush-type weather stripping to the bottom of the top half of the door where it won't show when half the door is open. Cheap foam rubber weather stripping won't hold up around so much traffic.

A ½-inch bevel on the outside of the bottom half of the door will help lead water out of the crack between the halves. Seal both door halves with as much water-sealer as they will absorb. In the case of the upright stiles on either side of the door, this will be quite a bit.

If the cross member is less than 8 inches, you should beef it up to make two strong half doors. A 1×2 glued with brown glue and screwed to the bottom of the upper door is adequate. Use 2-inch screws into the stiles. Screws measuring 1½ inches will do on the crossmember to pull the 1×2 tight until the glue dries. Cove molding dresses the joint inside and out. Butter it with brown glue before nailing it to the outside to assure that water doesn't run behind it where it won't dry.

The bottom half of the door should get a ledge for leaning

This Dutch door was made by cutting it apart at the cross member and adding a ledge.

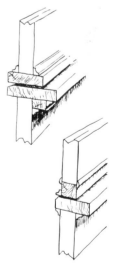

Two possible configurations for a Dutch door: any system that strengthens the door, provides a ledge, and controls water runoff will do the job.

Copper flashing should project from behind these old sash windows to lead water away. Flash from under the shingles over the top trim piece and under the bottom sash if the sill has no slant. To avoid having the exposed caulk degenerate in the sun cover it with tar paper. Galvanized flashing will add rust streaks which might be difficult to remove from glass without scratching.

The drawings below show three different fixed-glass windows.

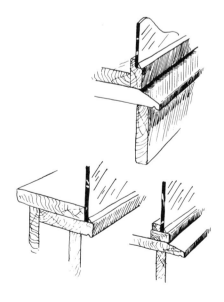

elbows. It doesn't need it, but then you didn't need to make a Dutch door in the first place, and you may as well do it right.

Use five-quarter stock for the ledge; one-by stock is too light for exterior use (except on façades) and two-by looks clumsy. Slope the outside edge so water won't come in the crack. If there's room for it, a strip of 1×2 can support the ledge, but it isn't absolutely necessary. Glue and screw the ledge. Use brass screws for this job if you want the screw heads to show, or cover the screw heads with plugs. Trim all ugly cracks with molding.

If the cross member is so narrow that the ledge and molding seem out of place, use 2×2 which is the same width as most doors. Trim the crack with half-round molding.

Any projection on the outside of the door will have to be rounded on the knob side to avoid hitting the frame when the door is closed. Round the molding also and shorten it a bit to provide a logical step pattern.

A throw bolt connecting the two halves of the door will allow you to open and close it as a unit.

Fixed windows can be set without a sash if the rest of the room is functional modern or wood-butcher in style. The job is too informal to look right in most pre-World War II rooms. A frame of one-by stock with, cedar shingles nailed to double studs and a header will do in these homes. Set the glass inside this with a ring of 1×2 on both sides to hold it in place. The rest of the job consists of keeping the window from rattling or leaking.

Prenail the 1×2-inch trim so the points of the nails just show on the bottom side. Don't let them project or they'll throw the trim out of line as it is put in place. If you should set a nail too far through the trim piece, pound it back so it sits flush; it won't become dull enough to cause a problem. Prenailing will free a hand to hold the trim in place and limit the hammer strokes near the glass.

Masking tape between the wood and the glass will help avoid rattles. Recess the tape so it doesn't show.

The sill usually extends past the window on each side to form a base for the vertical jamb that trims the window. The sill is cut out around the wall to do this. One-by or five-quarter stock is used. As the cut out edges are covered, making the cut freehand with a circular saw will do. The inside corners of the cut will have to be finished with a handsaw.

Normally a horizontal plate nailed to the wall under the sill appears to support it. The sill provides the bottom inside frame for the glass or sash.

The outer sill will direct water away from the house if it is given a bevel extending to just under the outside trim on the window. If less than 1 inch is involved, this bevel can be milled with a plane. If more than 1 inch needs to be beveled, a table saw is required.

A shallow V-shaped dado on the bottom of the outer sill will cause water to drip out near the edge of the sill before it has a chance to run under the siding of the house. The drip line can

This simple frame was used to set the salvaged windows for the kitchen on page 87.

be cut with two passes of the circular saw set at 45 degrees. The dado need not be neat but should be treated with a water-sealer.

Glaze the outside of the window to eliminate rattle and form a water-tight seal between the glass and the outside trim. Water sometimes runs down the glass in sheets. This should go over the outside trim and onto the slant in the outer sill.

To keep the glaze from showing from the inside of the window, the outside strip around the glass should be at least ½ inch lower than the inside strip.

You can use a 5/4×2 set on edge with a dado for the glass and glaze forms a frame that looks very similar to a sash. The dado must be cut on a table saw. Using 1×2 around the glass with a 1×1 strip on the inside works well and can be set with hand tools. Anyway you can raise the inside strip to hide the glaze will do the job.

To glaze glass roll the glaze as it comes from the can into a snake and press with your fingers to form a tight seal between the glass and the wood. First press the glaze in place and then smooth it with a broadknife. Glaze sticks better to painted wood than to raw, and water runoff is better on painted wood. If your design calls for a natural finish, paint the wood with clear watersealer. It will age more slowly than the unfinished wood around it, but this will show only on the inner part of the window and the contrast will add interest.

Glaze is not tremendously sticky. It will tend to pull away from the wood or the glass as you are working it. A coat of mineral oil on the wood will thin the glaze as they meet and will improve adhesion. A bit of oil on your finger also helps smooth the surface of the glaze.

Glaze dries and shrinks over a period of years but maintains enough cohesion to stay in place as long as it isn't broken. When replacing glaze, remove all the old glaze and scrape the frame clean. Patches of new and old glaze will not hold up.

Heat from a butane torch will soften old glaze for removal. So will tip tanks if you have the window stripped of paint but you must pick the window up before the glaze has a chance to dry out again.

Glazing pins are used to hold glass in place until the glaze is set. Triangles of sharp tin about ½ inch to a side can be bought in most hardware stores, but you can cut your own out of a can if it saves a trip. Paint cans are a little thicker than soup cans and make a better pin. Straighten the lead corner before pushing the pin down with a screwdriver.

Condensation is not usually a problem except in kitchens and bathrooms but large windows will chill a continuous blanket of air which then slides down the window and across the floor.

Double glass on large windows will prevent this. Separate the two panes as far as is feasible with 1×2 or 1×3 or even 1×4 and frame like a single pane window. An airtight seal isn't necessary or even desirable, although the job must be tight enough to keep insects out. All wood around a window should be sealed to avoid discoloration even though condensation will be slight.

Used-sash windows without the frame are the easiest old house parts to find. Often they can be had with fancy woodwork or lead caming for less than the price of plate glass the same size.

A fixed-sash window is set against an inner ring of wood which stops air from coming in around the sash. The window may be nailed in place and caulked or held by an outer ring. The bottom strip of wood should be omitted on the outer ring to improve water runoff.

Very fancy lead-camed windows placed up high are easier to clean safely if you add a pane of clear glass outside the sash. Many of these old windows won't take the pressure from a garden hose and washing them with a brush on the end of a stick is too risky.

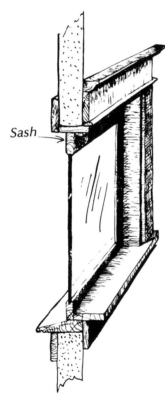

Sash

The sash window may be hinged or fixed.

Any old sash window can be mounted in a sliding frame if the wood is sound. The center separating bead sits in a dado. The rest of the tract is formed by the windowsill on the inside and a strip of wood on the outside.

A hinged window is set like a fixed window against an inner ring of wood. Use long-tongued strap hinges to hang it from the side. The metal screws into three of the four pieces that make up the sash for better support.

Windows hinged from the top should hang from the stiles on the side of the sash. If the sash is rotted or dried out, have it replaced by a window shop. Lead-camed glass is set in a dado and glazed like a single pane. Replacement of the sash presents no special problems.

Most double-hung windows have a lip on the bottom of the top sash which matches a lip on the top of the bottom sash when the window is closed to prevent drafts. If you can turn the windows sideways to make sliding windows, you can use the original setup. If you use the windows right side up, you will have to plane the lip off and add a piece to fill the gap where the windows are separated by parting bead.

The sill forms the inside edge of the first tract for sliding windows. Use parting bead or rip a piece of ½-inch stock 1-inch wide for the middle track. The windows will work more smoothly if the parting strip is dadoed in place so it can't shift. The outside track should be 2 inches short on both ends for drainage and so the track can clear itself of debris while the window slides back and forth.

More people have trouble with *skylights* than with any other remodeling project. Water running down the roof will seep under the shingles around any interruption in the roof unless the flashing extends up under two or more courses. Tar or

Skylight Frame

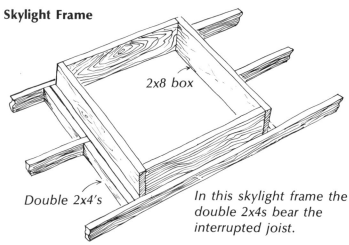

2x8 box

Double 2x4's

In this skylight frame the double 2x4s bear the interrupted joist.

This window complex is built of structural 2x4s filled by glass panes set in frames of 1x2. This entire unit cost $40 to build.

other roofing compounds will not do a permanent job of keeping water out. Capillary action will suck water up narrow spaces in the flashing if it has open seams. Perverse winds will blow water uphill to find weak spots around the glass. And even if the job is absolutely tight, condensation on the inside of the glass will drip like a leak when the weather gets cold. The smallest leak is enough to discolor your woodwork or stain the ceiling, turning what should be one of your proudest jobs into a persistent snivelling irritation.

On the other hand, skylight carpentry is not difficult and the results can be spectacular. Because a skylight stands alone on the ceiling clear of other moldings or architectural detail, it can be added even to a period house without doing damage to the house's character. Purists will snear but you'll have light where you didn't have light before.

The job is straight-forward while you are reroofing. It can be done with existing roofing if the shakes or shingles are still flexible enough to lift so that the flashing can be set.

If the room is a converted attic with the ceiling on the bottom of the same joists that hold the roof, the skylight frame is a simple box of 2×8 that projects above the roof line. If the room has an attic or crawl space between the ceiling and the roof, two boxes are built, one for the ceiling and one for the roof, with a light well connecting them.

You can safely cut one rafter, making an opening 30½ inches wide. The interrupted rafter should be supported at both ends of the opening by double 2×4s. Skylights wider than 30½ can be made by leaving the rafters in place and trimming them out to show. The opening can be as long in the direction of the joists as you like without structural problems.

Plasterboard ceilings will be found in most rooms that were built or remodeled after World War II when plasterboard came into common use. Cutting the opening is easy. Locate the joists by poking holes through the ceiling with a screwdriver and cut the plasterboard away with a razor knife.

Lath and plaster ceilings are more difficult. The wooden lath must be cut neatly without disturbance or you risk knocking loose large chunks of ceiling plaster that you don't want to lose. Poke a hole between the lath carefully with a screwdriver. Or locate the joists from the crawlspace and scratch your way through the plaster to mark the ceiling. Don't poke down or you'll knock chunks of plaster loose.

Nail every inch along the rafter with large headed roofing nails to be sure the lath and plaster is securely fastened. Set the nails flush but not inset into the plaster. Inset nails shatter the plaster and provide little holding power.

Saw out the opening just inside the rafters with a circular saw using an old blade. A saber saw moves too slowly and is liable to tear the lath loose. Before making the cut it is a good idea to scribe the plaster deeply with a razor knife so that if the section of ceiling plaster falls before you are done with the cut, it will have a place to break off. You'll be working over your head and making a lot of mess, so wear goggles, cover your head and keep your top shirt button buttoned. Seal off the area.

If you cut away a rafter to make a wider skylight, the rafter must be supported at both ends by double 2×4s. As the cut will be freehand and likely to be ugly, nestle the ends of the interrupted rafter between short lengths of 2×4.

If there is no crawl space, the double 2×4s must be placed from below. Cut lath and plaster back to the next rafter on each side to get room to work and splice back with wallboard. If the ceiling is wallboard, you can cut an opening at each end of the double 2×4s small enough to be covered by trim but large enough to screw the double 2×4s in place at a diagonal as though you were toenailing. This cannot be done with lath and plaster because lath cannot be cut except at a joist.

If the room has an attic, mark the roof directly above the ceiling opening, using a framing square or a plumb bob. Any weight on a light string will make a fine plumb bob.

It is a good idea to lay down boards to spread your weight across several rafters while you work in the attic.

Drill through the roof from below to establish the four corners of the opening. Cut out with a circular saw using an old blade. Asphalt shingles will leave a tarry residue on your blade. Clean this off with gasoline.

If the ceiling and roof rafters don't line up, add lumber to both sets of rafters until you make a narrower opening that does line up.

Before setting the 2×8 box which will hold the skylight, lift the shingles above and on both sides of the opening. Pick a warm day. Start about four courses above the opening and lift the first course a small amount of prying up the nails with a flat pry bar. Lift the next row a bit more until the last two rows can be removed entirely. Shingles at the sides are easier to lift because you have good access from the opening. Lift these back 12 inches.

The flashing should extend 1 foot in all four directions, under the shingles on the top and sides; above the shingles on the bottom. If the roofing deteriorates in the lifting, you will

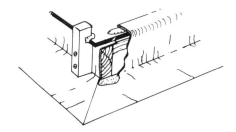

This is a detail of the lower end of a fixed skylight. You should caulk anywhere the glass touches.

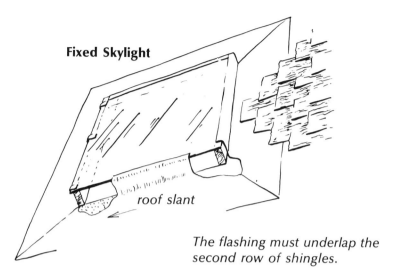

Fixed Skylight

roof slant

The flashing must underlap the second row of shingles.

have to replace it, which is apt to mean a new roof, so take a good look at your shingles before starting. You can cheat by removing the shingles entirely and covering the flashing with tar but the job may leak right away. It will surely leak in a few years when the tar dries out in the sun.

Set a box of 2×8 in the roof to frame the new skylight; 1 by 8 is too thin to be exposed. Five-quarter is adequate. In a room without an attic, the bottom of the box should be set level with the ceiling so the trim can be nailed to it. In a room with an attic a second frame, of 2×4, will have to be set so that the two openings remain the same size. Add upright 2×4 studs to frame the lightwell.

The *flashing* (also called the roof safe) should rise to the top of the skylight frame over the glass, and across the top of the glass ¾ inch or so. When figuring the rise, measure from the subroofing below the shingles to the top of the wood frame and the glass, and add ¼ inch or so to allow a pad of caulk above and below the glass. The safe should project 12 inches in all four directions.

Have the roof safe custom made by a metal shop. The bends should be crisp without buckles that will keep the safe from laying perfectly flat. The joints should be soldered and the zinc should be replaced where the heat melts it away. Paint on zinc will do the job if you solder your own joints with a torch.

Lay a bed of caulk evenly around the top of the box. Use ⅛ by ½ butyl caulk strips to get an even layer. Place the glass and lay a second bead of caulk on top of it. Set the roof safe and tar its top and side edges if you can get to them. Wear gloves and use a stick to apply black roof pitch directly from the can. On windy days streamers of tar will blow across the roof as it dribbles from the stick. Lay the shingles back down, starting at the bottom. Paste a dollop of roof patch under any shingles that don't lie back down smoothly. Tar over the shingles around the safe.

Building codes in some areas will require you to use glass with wire in it or plexiglass for a skylight. Eighth-inch plexiglass is adequate if the joists are left in place. Quarter-inch can span

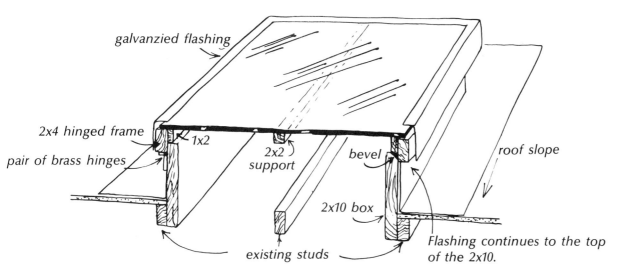

galvanzied flashing

2x4 hinged frame

1x2

pair of brass hinges

2x2
support

bevel

roof slope

2x10 box

existing studs

Flashing continues to the top
of the 2x10.

Opening Skylight

*Make this skylight so that it
opens away from the prevailing
breeze, letting heat escape but
not catching a chill wind. You
should caulk above and below
the glass and above the 2x2
center support. The lower end
(not shown here) is finished
just as the fixed skylight is, as
shown on page 67.*

farther but is four times as expensive. Some areas will allow the
use of tempered safety glass. Others will not. Check with your
county building inspector if the job can be seen from the road.

The glass projects on the lower end for water runoff. To
keep it from sliding out of its frame, use tabs of sheet metal
from the roof safe, or build wood holders lined with caulk.

An opening skylight can be made with a simple change in
design. The box must project higher to allow a 2×4 cap to sit
atop it. An opening skylight lets heat escape—it doesn't let
breezes in. Set in to open away from the prevailing breeze if
you have one and design the stick that raises it so that it will
also keep the skylight from catching a breeze and flopping
completely open.

Condensation is a problem in any room if it gets cold enough
outside and especially bad in bathrooms and kitchens where
hot humid air hits the cold glass. Double glass will not solve
the problem entirely but it will cut it to a minimum. The second
piece of glass can sit in a dado two inches below the top glass
in a fixed or opening skylight. Make the dado oversize and
pack caulk above and below the glass to keep the wood from
soaking up water. A ring of 1×2 can hold the glass. In this case
the top of the glass should be fastened in place with glazing
pins so it doesn't move when the light is opened. Caulk the
perimeter with silicone bathtub caulk over painted wood. If
the skylight does not open, the glass may be set at ceiling
height and held in place by the trim around the light well.

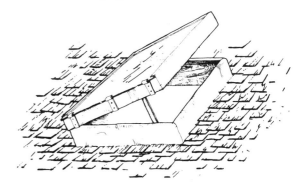

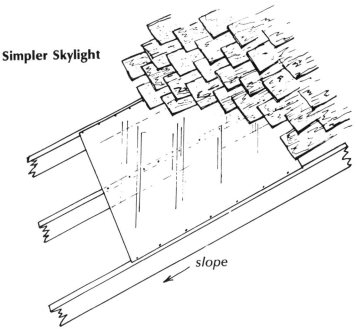

Simpler Skylight

slope

The plex or filon in this skylight cannot be replaced after installation.

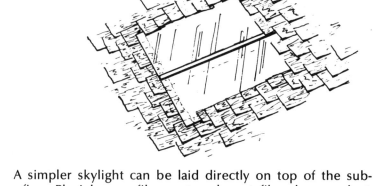

A simpler skylight can be laid directly on top of the subroofing. Plexiglass or filon, a translucent fiberglass product, will do the job. Lay under two or three courses of shingles on the sides and top to assure that leaks between the shingles can't get under the skylight. Tar the edges in lieu of flashing. Nail every 6 to 8 inches along rafters that run through the light. Tar the nail heads and cover with a wood batt of 1×2 or ½×2 to protect the tar. Drill plexiglass before nailing.

A skylight of plex or filon can extend to any distance across rafters but cannot be easily replaced when it gets etched and dirty looking, so hold yourself to greenhouses or eaves where the light passes into a window underneath.

Patented bubble domes are available from a range of manufacturers and solve some typical skylight problems. Manufacturers' literature usually recommends "curb mounting" their skylights on a box as described for roofs with less than 3:12 pitch. A lip is molded into the plex to go over the edge of the box and eliminate a flashing problem. The box must still be flashed under the roofing material.

For roofs steeper than 3:12, flush mounted lights are offered. The dome shape helps avoid dirt and loadup of leaves and needles from nearby trees which are the major problems with flush mounted skylights.

Bubbles are offered in double layers with flat plexiglass on the inside layer of lights smaller than 24 inches. Curved plex is used on the inner bubble on larger models. A two-inch air space between the bubbles insulates and controls condensation.

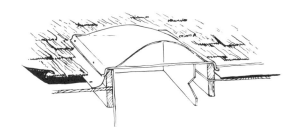

Some condensation will still result, even with double bubble domes. The best models recognize this fact with gutters on the inside of their frames.

Double dome skylights start at about $25 for the smallest sizes and run up to nearly $200. A typical 32×48 lists for $125. Single domes run about 25 percent less. Clear and white-frosted lights are common.

Use a curb-mounted bubble to make an opening skylight and frame as you would a homemade light.

Normal skylight problems were avoided with this second story lightwell which leads to an attic window. Ceiling joists were trimmed and left uninterrupted. Vents were added to the attic to make up for lost air circulation.

REFINISHING OLD WOOD: FROM STRIPPING TO THE GLOWING FINISH

Stripping a fifty-year accumulation of paint off old wood with liquid paint stripper is slow, boring work. Get out of it if you can. Hire kids to do it or remove the pieces from the wall and send them to a dip tank. Look into removing the paint mechanically, with heat or a power sander, especially with cedar or redwood, which will discolor in dip tanks.

Chip away a bit of paint from any piece that you are considering refinishing and look for varnish underneath. Dark brown or red pigmented varnish is common in houses built from about the turn-of-the-century until World War II—as long as wood was a major design element. Varnish softens readily and comes off well with liquid hand-stripper or in a dip tank, leaving dark stains in cracks and corners that cannot be completely removed. The dark stains do give a pleasant antique color modulation to the job when it is refinished and completed.

If you don't find varnish under the paint, the wood was painted originally and is a poor candidate for natural refinishing. Instead of pleasing dark stains in the hard to reach areas, you will be left with paint seeped into the wood. This is impossible to remove. Even large flat surfaces, such as Wainscottings, strip poorly if they were painted originally.

Check both the panels and stiles of doors before deciding to strip them. Manufacturers carried in their catalogs a wide variety of doors, making them up from shelved components. Fir stiles with redwood inserts, for instance, are common in doors sold in the San Francisco area between 1890 and 1900 and other combinations of wood aren't uncommon. The aged redwood will be much darker than the fir stiles, which isn't a bad effect, but is disconcerting if it wasn't what you had in mind. The only way you will be able to bring them to any semblance of period work is by staining the lighter fir very dark.

Victorians often varnished the woodwork in public rooms and painted it upstairs and in the private back room such as the kitchen and pantry. The entry foyer, stair banister, front parlor trim, dining room Wainscotting and sometimes the woodwork in the master bedroom were often varnished. For this woodwork, hardwoods or high-quality softwoods were used. For the woodwork in other bedrooms, bathrooms, kitchen and pantry, lesser grades and mixed woods were used. Because this wood was originally painted, the carpenter was allowed to use more putty, plaster and gesso. Doors and windows were often painted.

After World War I, woodwork got to be nearly a fetish in some interiors. False beam ceilings came into vogue. Wainscotting rose to eye level and became plainer. Doors and window sashes that would have been painted in Victorian times were often varnished. Much of this wood was varnished very dark.

Woodwork that is still varnished but is unattractive under layers of grime and drips of paint from the surrounding walls can be restored without stripping back to the wood. As the oils

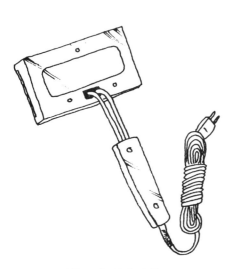

Electric Paint Remover

dry out of varnish, it shrinks into irregular islands. Adhesion to the wood isn't impaired and flaking or peeling is rare. Alligatored varnish is honest and hard-earned, like grey hair and wrinkles, and ought to be preserved.

Clean alligatored, darkened varnish with Tri-Sodium Phosphate, which is available in most hardware stores in a grainy powder advertised for cleaning driveways. Mixed with water TSP forms a mild paint stripper that will soften varnish. Scrape paint slop off the varnished wood with a dull metal edge and paint on a coat of TSP and water. Clean the broad areas that are not dappled with paint slop with TSP on a damp rag, using the TSP as you would sink cleanser. Most of the grime will disappear without removing any more of the alligatored varnish than necessary. As this job is messy, it should be done right before you paint the wall.

Neutralize the base TSP with vinegar and water before giving the wood a new coat of varnish. Also clean any wall area that has gotten TSP slopped on it so that it doesn't affect your paint job. Allow the job to dry completely and apply pigment-bearing varnish to match the old. You can use lighter varnish if you wipe-stain the areas that you have scrubbed down to the wood.

Dark finishes that don't respond to TSP or denatured alcohol may be lacquered. Try cleaning them with benzene and neutralize afterward with soap and water.

Light-colored alligatored wood may have been varnished or shellacked; shellac was frequently used in areas away from hand traffic. If the finish does not respond to TSP, it is probably shellac. Clean this with denatured alcohol, which softens it. Neutralize with detergent and water, and apply new shellac or varnish. As shellac softens on humid days, it shouldn't be used on doors or frames where people will bump into it.

Woodwork that gets a lot of traffic also gets a lot of paint. If the paint is very thick, you'll waste a lot of time and paint stripper getting it off. Sometimes though it chips away easily. Latex chips best. Thin paint doesn't chip well. This job is messy but fun; chips of paint fly all over the place. The front edge of a jack plane does a fine job (don't use the blade which will cut into the wood). Any stiff dull metal edge will do. Don't use a patented paint scraper on wood you want to finish natural or you will cut below the patina in places and produce an irregular finish. Clean up the job with a light coat of liquid paint stripper.

Plaster of Paris ornaments don't hold paint well and are good candidates for paint chipping. The surface of plaster will often part neatly with the paint, leaving a smooth clean surface underneath. Paint stripper produces a gooey mess that makes unnecessary work. Use it on plaster only when chipping and digging fails. Plaster cannot be dip-tanked because it soaks up water and decomposes.

Heavy paint on irregular surfaces that do not chip readily can be softened with a butane torch. *Burning* is usually limited to wood that will be repainted but you can soften very heavy paint without damaging the wood. Hold the heat to the paint

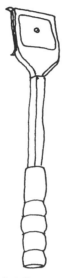

Paint Scraper

This stairway has seen a great deal of traffic over the years and has received many layers of paint. Thick paint will often chip off easily but the bannisters and other pieces that have much detail would take more readily to being dismantled and dipped.

just long enough for it to bubble and follow quickly with a broadknife or other scraping tool. You don't want to leave burns on the wood, so don't scrape all of the softened paint away. Leave a border to protect the wood while you burn the next segment. Avoid heating chipped or worn areas where the paint is thin. The torch can be aimed very precisely so avoiding thin spots is easy. Work very small segments so that you can get them stripped before they cool.

Bright high-temperature *lamps* are available for stripping paint but these are more expensive than butane torches and cannot be as tightly aimed. They shouldn't be used on wood that you wish to finish natural.

Electric heater-type paint strippers should be used only on wood that will be painted afterward. These are designed to rest on the wood and leave burn marks.

After chipping or burning, the job will clean up with liquid hand stripper.

Dip tanks are of limited use to the house restorer because they are harsh and because most of the wood you want to strip cannot be removed from the wall without damage. Stripping by hand is much work and dipping is relatively cheap, so some pieces (especially those that are going to be repainted so that you can repair splits or other damage) might be removed and dipped.

The pieces most often dipped are doors because they are most easily removed. Bevelled or etched glass that can't be easily replaced should be removed before the door is dipped or they may be broken as the wood swells and contracts in dipping and drying. Glue joints are not attacked by the stripper but if they are in poor condition, this will become obvious when the paint is removed. The door must be well-sealed and finished afterward or it will swell and shrink with changes in atmospheric moisture.

Windows are usually dipped with the sash and glass left intact. The sash hasn't enough heft to shift around and break the glass as a door might. The glazing compound will soften in the dip tank and harden again as it dries. This is a good time to remove and renew it but you must arrange to pick up the window soon after it is dipped. The chemicals in the dip tanks will not etch your glass.

Kickplates, jambs and other trim are usually so hard to remove that this job is best done only during a total remodeling so that the wall can be gouged if necessary to minimize damage to the wood. As the nails are often frozen into ancient fir studs, they will have to be pulled through the wood as it is pried away from the wall.

Old fir trim is very hard and brittle. Never pull on the trim piece itself, regardless of how much is already free. Pry the top or one side of the piece from the wall along its entire length. Set the straight end of your pry bar as far down between the loosened trim and the stud as possible and insert a small block of wood as a fulcrum for prying out the bottom or far side. Pry as near the nail as you can.

Use steel wool for hand-stripping irregular surfaces. In this house doors and window sashes were stripped, frames and moldings were left painted.

Regardless of how careful you are, you must figure on some loss to splitting in removing antique wood, and additional loss in the dip tank due to curl and splitting. If you want to restore your interior without giving up the trim in one room for replacement parts in the other rooms, strip your wood by hand.

Dip plants maintain two kinds of baths, the cold tank, which is gentle but expensive and used mostly for fine furniture, and the hot tank, which is used for most soft woods.

The cold tank contains a solution of methylene chloride, the same ingredient used in hand strippers. Methylene chloride breaks down the chemical structure of the paint so that it will wash away with a scrub brush. Lacquer in solution in the cold tank will sometimes leave a pink tint on the wood especially fir, pine and hemlock if the bath isn't clean. Some plants rinse the wood with lacquer thinner after it has been dipped. Most use water, which does a good job.

The hot tank contains a solution of caustic soda—lye—which eats away the paint rather than breaking it down. Most softwood and anything heavily painted is stripped in the hot tank. After stripping, the piece is neutralized in a mild acid bath of oxalic acid. Lye left on the piece would make soap out of the new finish.

Lye baths have two disadvantages. Lye will darken redwood to a deep brown and leach out yellows and reds. Maple stain will put the red and yellow back in but as you are starting with a dark color before you stain, you will end up with a very dark wood. Spar varnish is good for putting highlights and some color back into stripped redwood. In this case you will want to finish the other wood in the room in spar varnish except where water will touch it.

Lye baths will also darken fir and hemlock but not enough to be a problem. To check the species of wood, scrape a large enough area down to raw wood to check the grain. Redwood or cedar will be a dark brown or orange and soft enough to crease with your fingernail. Fir ages to a medium golden brown with distinct ridges of hard and soft grain. The hard grain can't be creased with a fingernail; the soft grain can only with difficulty. Hemlock is similar to fir, usually with a slightly less distinct grain, lighter color and softer texture. Pine is soft and creamy white with very little noticeable grain. Pine is very susceptible to picking up stains in the tank but will also pick up the most stain when you refinish the wood so this causes little problem.

The second problem with lye tanks is that lye will attack the lignin that holds the wood fiber together. Open-face grain will sometimes rise up and separate, leaving you with a touchy gluing problem. If you have grain to glue back down, do so after you apply the stain and first coat of finish so glue-slop doesn't prevent part of the wood from coloring. Use contact cement on raised grain.

After dipping in either tank the piece must dry for a week before a new finish is applied. To prevent warping while the moisture dries out of the wood, the pieces should be kept out

Lye baths affect different woods in special ways. This might be a problem when stripping a piece such as this door that is made up of several different species of wood.

Be certain to finish stripping the details in the woodwork as you go. Otherwise you'll rediscover them as you start the finishing.

of the sun. Doors must stand straight or lie flat with supports every two or three feet. Long boards can lean against a wall. Warpage along the length of the board isn't a problem as nails will pull it flat. Bows across the grain are critical and have to be taken out with weights.

A white film will dry on the surface of pieces dipped in either the hot or cold tanks. This comes off quickly with steel wool or sandpaper. The grain will also stand up, making some pieces as fuzzy as a short-hair cat. These come off quickly with sanding and cause no real damage. But don't be too surprised if you have to do some detail stripping by hand after you get the piece back.

If you intend to Dutch a door or rip it vertically for use in a tight space or make other alterations, do it after dipping.

Hand stripping is the solution of last resort. After you've checked for varnish and found it underneath the paint, chipped or burned away as much as possible, take the rest away with hand stripper. Limit yourself to small succinct projects. If you attack your entryway and living room all at once, kickplate, window and door jambs, stair banister, pillars and Wainscotting, you'll burn out before the job is properly done.

The details *must* be done as you go. Later never comes in renovation projects. Priority on jobs that are 95 percent complete falls below other jobs that haven't been started yet. It will be years before you get back to the paint left in cracks and corners. Meanwhile you don't have a wood-trimmed room but a room of painted wood that calls attention to the fact that it has been stripped.

Paint stripper contains methylene chloride, the same chemical used to break down the structure of paint in the cold dip tanks. It will also break down the polymers in a plastic tarp and soak through old sheets, so cover the floor with three or four layers of newspaper before you start. The newspapers will roll up, carrying the mess with them and making clean-up easy. Changing the newspapers once or twice during the job will help contain the mess.

Whenever you're doing a job by hand, buy the best materials available. The most expensive strippers are nearly as thick as yogurt and sell for about $13 a gallon in hardware stores. One side of a heavily painted and unchipped door will use about a pint of stripper and take 4 to 6 hours to strip.

Pour the stripper into a glass bowl and paint it over the first surface of the piece you're stripping. (If you use an old paint brush, you'll be pleased to see it come back to life.) The paint on the surface will begin to alligator almost immediately. Add stripper to the dry areas as they appear. In five minutes you'll be able to scrape the old finish away with a broadknife or pancake turner. The surface usually comes about 80 percent clean in the first stripping.

Repeat the process. The second coat of stripper will still be moist when you scrape it off. Reuse it on the next area to be stripped; paint stripper isn't dead until it's dry.

After the surface is clean of most finish, give it a final light coat, stacking the stripper in cracks and crevices. Let this set twenty minutes to soften the hard-to-get places. Scrape again and go after the details with whatever is handy. The backside of a pocketknife blade works well at getting into cracks. A butterknife is good for inside rounds. Steel wool will handle the rest. You won't get all of the old finish out of cracks but you don't need to. The new finish will fill the cracks and cover any paint left behind. If the new finish is clear or light tint, you can cheat by coloring the paint left in deep cracks with a sharply pointed felt-tip pen.

Oak is a heavily pitted wood. These pits can be left full of the original dark varnish or they can be cleaned with a soft wire brush of the sort that welders use to clean slag or surgeons use on their fingernails. Cleaning the pits in oak is a fine point as you're going to fill them back up with new finish that will look a lot like the old.

Rub the irregular areas with medium-fine steel wool and

Both of these medicine cabinets were made by adding mirrors to salvaged materials. The door shown above was originally part of a sideboard and was turned upside down. The mirror replaced the large unleaded glass but the leaded panes below were left in place. The back of the cabinet was tiled with mirrored squares.

This tub was set in an alcove off the main room of this woodbutcher house and it has become the visual center of the room. The old claw-legged tub was painted charcoal gray on the outside; its plumbing is simple.

sand the flat surfaces with 100-grit sandpaper. Unless the piece has been badly abused and has ragged spots, the sanding will go quickly. You are simply removing dry stripper and polishing the wood.

Irregular surfaces such as the molding around the glass or surrounding a panel in a door can be scraped with whatever is handy. A dessert spoon works well as does a butterknife. Take the rest down with steel wool using a sloppy piece to push the wet stripper ahead and a clean piece for polishing. You're supposed to be wearing rubber gloves when working with liquid hand stripper but most people don't because they are so uncomfortable. The skin on your hands is tough enough if they aren't raw. You'll know it right away if you get stripper on the skin of your arm; it'll burn. Wash it off when that happens with soap and water.

Deep scratches in the wood will have to be left in. They add character. Cigarette burns or discolorations can be removed with a paint scraper. (A paint scraper is a sharp tool that you pull toward yourself to remove curls of paint; about $3.) Small areas of pigment residue, where the varnish was in poor condition before the paint was applied, can also be scraped clean. The scraper works well on vertical grain but poorly on open-faced wood where it will remove soft grain faster than hard grain and result in caterwauling. Don't let the corner dig in or you'll leave ridges.

After you scrape, feather the job with steel wool or 100-grit sandpaper and experiment with light or medium tone wipe stains to blend the scraped area with the aged wood around it.

Finishing wood is the payoff: the grain will come out; the wood will take on a nice glow, and if your joints don't glare too badly, the cabinet will suddenly look like a permanent part of the house. Your range of finishes includes plastic resin, which dries inside the wood; and oils, which don't dry at all but which won't crack or scratch either. Each of these finishes can be had clear or tinted with stain.

Plastic resin oil is easy to use because you paint it on and wipe off the excess, which eliminates problems with runs and dust. To produce a hand-rubbed finish, allow the first coat to dry and sand off the wood fibers that stand to attention with 120-grit sandpaper. These rise only on the first coat. The second and third coats (if the piece gets a third coat) are painted on and rubbed in with 600-grit wet-and-dry sandpaper. The sanding goes rapidly and produces a glowing soft finish. Sand until the finish goes dry (about a minute per yard on loose 1×4). Polish with paper towels to get off what is left. Low spots and crevices will get less rubbing and shine less, which keeps the job from looking like molded plastic.

Pieces which are nailed to the wall separately around doors or windows or floors can be completely finished before being nailed up. Cabinet trim can get the first coat before being nailed to the cabinet. This will allow you to paint both sides as a check against warping and keep any glue seepage from affecting your stain job. Second and third coats should be applied after the cabinet is assembled (although it needn't yet be

Both ends of the cedar Wainscotting in this bathroom are covered and can be rough cut with a circular saw without showing. A ½-inch strip of fir fills the gap between the horizontal 1x4 and the wall. The fir and cedar were finished with Olympic cedar stain. The mirror in this case was glued directly onto the wall with mastic (but this is risky because the silvering might have come off the glass). A strip of masonite to raise the two vertical frame pieces might have worked better.

hung) so you can control the overall color match. Stain is best applied to fir or hemlock after the first coat of finish to avoid blotches.

Some people claim that clear plastic resin doesn't block ultraviolet rays and that it shouldn't be used on the exterior (regardless of what the can says) because ultraviolet will attack the bond between the finish and the wood. This may be a prejudice against a product simply because it is new. Verithane produces a thinner coat of finish than does varnish or lacquer and may not seal the crevices in the door as well, allowing moisture to seep in. The result is a door that changes size with the weather.

Where you need a thicker finish to fill cracks in a door that has been dipped or where your work is near old work that has a shiny superficial finish, use *varnish*. New varnish can be "brought down" by a light polishing with very fine steel wool. Don't get carried away or you'll dull the job. Varnish is soft. Bring it back up with paste wax.

Use a top quality hair brush for varnish and apply just enough for the brushstrokes to join and form a smooth film. Apply the wet brush to a new area a small distance from the area you just painted and feather the two together working the brushstrokes from the new to the old. Make the coat as thin as possible to avoid runs.

Drying time is affected by humidity and temperature and it in turn affects how much dust you will pick up so choose a warm, dry day to apply varnish.

Oils are the best choice for counters and table tops, that get a lot of wear, because they don't scratch or chip, and dings in the wood can be sanded out at any time. New oil will blend perfectly with the old. Oak, teak, beech or any hardwood can be finished with plastic resin or tung oil because the wood is hard enough to provide a surface for the hard finish. Any wood soft enough to crease with your fingernail when it is raw—

redwood, cedar, pine, alder—will crease if it gets a lot of traffic and cause a hard finish to crack and turn white.

Stain is absorbed faster by softwood than by harder wood. Pine absorbs a great deal but usually needs it because it is very light in color. Fir and hemlock vary and will sometimes take dark splotches for no apparent reason. Hemlock absorbs more stain than fir. As these two woods are sold interchangeably for trim, matching the color sometimes requires hand-staining in addition to whatever stain might be in the finish. Decks, handrails and other wood that will be stained as its only treatment should be of only one wood. With only one step, all you can do is allow the stain to seep longer on the fir to bring it as dark as the hemlock. The darker the stain, the worse the color match will be.

Interior woodwork gives you a bit more flexibility. To avoid blotches and give tighter control of the staining, paint the wood first with clear sealer or plastic resin and allow it to dry. After the first sanding, glue the cabinet together and apply stain. Allow the stain to seep for a moment and wipe off with rags or paper towels. Extra rubbing with a rag damp with paint thinner will give you tighter color control. Further modulation can be gotten with steel wool after the stain is dry.

Putty fills pores and alters the finish of the wood so putty nailholes as a very last step. Stick putty is the easiest to use and can be used only after the finish is completed. Rub it on like a crayon and wipe the excess away; it's available in many colors.

Plastic resins with stain simplify finishing although no one brand dominates the market the way Flecto Verithane dominates clear plastic oil. The tinted plastic is wiped on and rubbed off according to the needs of the piece. If some sanding is required, the second coat of oil will re-stain with perfect blending. More coats will darken the wood unnecessarily so switch to clear when the color is right.

Deft (or other brands of plastic resin which are applied and not wiped off) can be used as a final coat over any of the plastic resins. The result will be a higher gloss and thicker finish (even if matte is used) that is susceptible to dust while drying.

Tung oil hardens; some of the other furniture oils don't—but all are used the same way. Apply with 600-grit sandpaper for a hand-rubbed finish and renew occasionally by wiping it on, allowing it to seep in and then wiping away the excess.

Wood around water makes for a lot of problems and a lot of disagreement on how to handle them. Showers and sinks pick up a film of soap that doesn't wash off easily without abrasive cleansers. No finish is hard enough to stand up to abrasives for clean-up and no finish will indefinitely keep water from getting underneath it and discoloring the wood. A material other than wood is the best choice for shower stalls and around the bathroom sink.

If you do use wood counters in the bathroom, match the finish to the wood. On hardwoods or harder softwoods, such as fir or hemlock, a plastic resin finish works as well as any hard finish can near water because it dries in the wood rather than

This sink was custom-built from a copper mixing bowl and fit between the walls studs in this tiny half-bathroom. The finish on the oak is verathane.

Wood near water is difficult to take care of because abrasive cleansers can't be used on it. But a plastic resin finish will soak into the wood if its allowed to stand in the finish for a few extra minutes and will provide a smooth and hard surface.

on it and is thin enough to soak up well in endgrain. Any wood that ends near the sink or tub should stand in the plastic oil a few minutes in the first finishing to soak up as much finish as possible. Sand and re-coat twice to get as smooth and hard a surface as possible for cleaning.

The last coat of plastic resin can be painted on after the woodwork is installed. A line of clear silicone where the counter meets the wall will help control water absorption and make clean-up easier. The job will discolor over time.

The best treatment for softer woods used as counter tops is a coat of water sealer and repeated coats of tung oil renewed like furniture polish whenever the wood dries out enough that water doesn't bead up. To clean the counter when it really needs it, scrape and re-oil the way a butcher maintains his chopping block. A lemon squeezed onto the wood after it is scraped bleaches it a bit and sweetens the smell.

The alternative is to cover the counter in a thick fiberglass resin which defeats the whole purpose of having wood. Rather than try to make wood into something it never was, use formica and at least get a counter that won't etch and hold dirt.

The wall here is made of salvaged and belt-sanded redwood T&G with no stain and two coats of eggshell verathane. The towel rack is ¾" rigid copper pipe set in brackets cut out of 2x4.

Spar varnish is often used in bathrooms because it gets used extensively on boats and boats get used around water. But varnish turns white when the wood underneath gets wet, on a boat or in a bathroom. Yachtsmen sand and varnish their boats continually; don't use spar varnish in the bathroom unless you want to do the same.

Cedar showers are beautiful but provide greater problems than counter tops. Hard finishes are too brittle for use on such a soft wood. Sealer won't crack but it won't provide a washable surface. Skin oil and soap together make a tenacious crud and cedar-walled showers will show their age almost before they have any. Sealer and oil in repeated coats is about the best finish. The worst problems can be eliminated if the cedar stops several inches from the floor of the shower and has plenty of room around it to dry out.

Cedar panelling above the tub doesn't have the same problem because soapy water doesn't run down it. A single row of tiles along the top of the porcelain is enough to protect the area that needs frequent cleaning. Silicone the ends of the boards where they touch the tub before applying the tiles. Apply silicone above the tiles after they are laid. Seal the wood with water-sealer before putting it up.

Wood walls away from the water in a bathroom should get a

coat of water-sealer. The wood doesn't change color and little of the fresh cedar smell is lost.

Wood which will be repainted is so easy to prepare that it doesn't make sense to do less than a good job. Removing and cleaning up the hinges and other hardware on a door makes the difference between a job just *done* and one done very well. Remove the lightswitch and socket covers before you paint and discard ugly ones that have been painted before. You'll be repaid with pride every time you enter the room.

Wood that is heavily painted and has missing chips can be restored with Spackle. Clean the trim with soapy water and prime at least the chipped areas so the Spackle will stick well. If the door is painted with high-gloss enamel, paint primer over the entire woodwork.

Spackle comes pre-mixed to about the consistency and appearance of toothpaste and spreads easily with a putty knife or finger. A quick pass over the chips will fill them in. Smooth out the job with sandpaper and re-prime so that you can inspect the job. Sometimes a second Spackle job is needed. This also is a good time to scrape out and Spackle joints that aren't smooth.

The door between the kitchen and the dining room sometimes has so much paint on it that new chips will appear the first time it's bumped. Doors this heavily painted should be dip-stripped even though you will have to apply two or three coats of paint to make them look like the surrounding woodwork.

Walls can be prepared with Spackle in the same manner as the woodwork.

Watermarks on the wall can't be painted over until the source of the water has been found and fixed. Even if the water has long since been stopped and the wall is completely dry, watermarks will usually burn through the new paint. The standard procedure to prevent this is a coat of shellac but this will alligator on enamel and other nonporous surfaces. Artist's charcoal fixative or hair spray does a better job of keeping the brown line under the new paint.

Mildew and other discolorations should be cleaned thoroughly and sealed before the wall is painted. Don't panic if white paint doesn't look like the color chip when it first goes on. White paint turns translucent while it's drying and doesn't appear to cover. Darkly tinted latex enamel doesn't cover well. As many as four coats may be needed for kelly green to cover white enamel although other colors cover better. Use oil-based enamel for dark colors.

Paint is one of the industries that has not yet been taken over by giants. Paint factories are located in most cities and offer their product at $3 to $4 below national brands of the same quality. Inventories tend to be small and change so be sure the paint you are buying will be available if you need more to finish the job.

Paint factories will custom-tint paint and provide all of the services that come with the more expensive outlets. Tell the

Three salvaged doors were dip-stripped for this entryway. The window above the main door is a fixed pane set in wood strips and caulked. Note the redwood panels in the closet doors. The beveled glass in the oak front door was cracked during the stripping and drying process. This could have been avoided by removing it before stripping.

salesman that you are doing a "spec house" (a house done on speculation of profit rather than for a client) and ask for your rightful 20 percent professional discount. If you can keep a straight face, you'll probably get it.

Exterior wood isn't seen from up close and will take the roughest stripping methods when blistered or peeled paint must be removed. Blisters and peels are most common on the south side where the sun shines most of the day and in places that get damp. Sometimes blisters will form on the underlip of shiplap for no apparent reason. These must be scraped away. Dust and spider's egg balls that were painted in place on the previous jobs should also be removed.

Don't do any more work than necessary. Scraping or wire brushing will often do the job without removing unnecessary amounts of old paint. Wire brushing alone is used on shakes, shingles and other rough-hewn siding.

If the paint is badly blistered, you'll have to take it down to the wood for a smooth paint job. Limit this work to siding at eye level where details can be seen. Elsewhere, remove only what is loose.

A disk sander does the easiest and quickest job of removing old paint. The blade leaves swirls in the wood but these are shallow enough to fill with latex paint. Use 60-grit sandpaper. Figure about 100 square feet sanded per hour on shiplap with a heavy-duty disk sander. You'll actually go faster than 100 square-feet-per-hour but set-up time and breaks and distractions will slow you down.

A belt sander won't leave swirls in the wood but the belt will tear on the piece of shiplap above the one you are working. At $1.50 to $2 per belt, this gets old in a hurry.

Whenever you're doing heavy-duty sanding, wear a mask. Disposable paper masks are available in hardware stores and at tool rental outlets for about 50 cents. The models with disposable filter inserts fit the face better and exchange the air more fully. (They cost about $5.) Old air gets to be a major discomfort if you are not used to the masks and the extra air exchange of the better model is worth the money.

Eye protection should be worn while sanding paint. You'll be working in a cloud of tiny, sharp chips of paint.

If you don't have a heavy-duty sander and are doing the work evenings and weekends so a rental tool is inconvenient, burn the paint off. This job is scary and every once in a while a house is burned down by a person who gets careless and holds the heat in one place too long.

Heat softens the paint so that it can be scraped off. The scraping must follow the heat in short passes before the paint has a chance to cool. The very bright electric hot lamps are available for $20 at hardware and automotive supply houses. Electric-heater-type burners are cheaper but slower.

The butane torch, which is useful for many other jobs, does an economical job of stripping exterior paint. The spreader attachment, which comes with it if you buy a kit, is used for burning paint. A cannister of gas will burn the blistered area

The oak trim is finished with two coats of plastic resin oil. To control the splashing and soap buildup which is difficult to remove from woodwork water pressure is regulated at the cutoff valve. No soap is placed at the sink. Either formica or tile used as a slashboard would have cluttered the design but eased these restrictions.

on one side of a large house in a week of diligent summer evenings.

Spindles, moldings and gingerbread should be burned and sanded. Aim the torch at holes and depressions first using the paint on projecting parts to protect them. If you clean the top surface first, you'll burn the wood when you go at the inside sections.

Sand curved parts with a contour sander (about $25). Contour sanders are a round brush that pushes strips of sandpaper which conform to irregular shapes.

Burned areas which show should be scraped clean. The dry crumbs of burnt paint fall off rapidly. Hand sand with a block and Spackle as necessary for a smooth finish. Paint will fill nothing larger than an isolated scratch.

Wood that has been stripped clean should be primed before it's painted. Primer adheres to the wood better than heavy pigment-laden paint.

If blistering is heavy on the south side, prime the whole wall. Blistering sometimes occurs on the outside wall of bathrooms that have showers and aren't well-vented. If you are sure the blistering is not caused by a leak in the plumbing or the roof, and caulk is in good shape where rain might enter the wall, steam is your problem. Put a fan in the bathroom and install vents in the wall. The simplest vents insert into 1-inch holes drilled in the shiplap.

Bonding agents can be added to paint to increase its adherence in damp or excessively hot spots.

Eaves on old houses are hard to get to and will need a lot of attention because the previous owners of the house couldn't get to them any better than you can. Dry rot loves to accumulate where the sun doesn't shine. Huge, luxuriant blisters are common. As soon as you start scraping at the awkward struts and decoration around the eaves you'll be tempted to rent a sandblaster and airpump and blast the old paint away. Don't do this unless you're prepared to restore the rotten wood that is held together by the paint. This might very well require tearing up the roof if the bottom of the eave is the underside of the roof.

Eaves are good things to ignore as long as you can. They support nothing but themselves and the gutter and maybe they'll hold together until you sell the house. Tie a rope around your waist, give the other end to a hefty friend, lean out the window and scrape the part that shows from the room as everybody before you has done. Knock off the loose paint on the rest. You can't see the details from the ground.

The alternative is scaffolding. Sufficient metal scaffolding with planks to do the side of a two-story house costs about $60 a month. Two people are required for assembly or moving. If the eaves need work, gutters or the roof are going to get care, or extensive burning is required on the side of the house, scaffolding saves enough time over ladders to justify the extra expense. Extension ladders with racks for planks can also be rented.

KITCHENS: THE BIG JOB AT THE END OF THE LINE

Remodel your kitchen last. It is the most expensive job in the house and the one that demands the most thought. It requires the most experience at carpentry and the widest range of other skills and offers, in exchange, the best opportunity to really shine.

Give a lot of thought to what you want; the list of necessities for ending up with a successful kitchen is almost endless. If you entertain, a work space that allows you to face your first guests while you are still working might be desirable. Most parties do get started in the kitchen, after all.

If you have children who tend to drag home clay and feathers and *papier-mâché* volcanoes with red cellophane veins of lava, a crafts area or breakfast nook can help keep the overflow out of the main thoroughfare. The counters should be easy to wipe. Spices should be kept out of the sun. Rarely used utensils should be hung away from the stove where they will collect grease.

The sink requires counterspace on both sides for clean and dirty dishes with more space nearby to chop vegetables. The sink can also be used to hide splices in the formica if the counter rounds a corner.

A trash-burner in the kitchen will give you an excuse to expose an old brick chimney and stand by you when the blackouts come. In the meantime it will cut your garbage in half and get rid of onion scraps before they begin to smell. A washer and dryer in the kitchen will allow you to take care of your laundry while you cook.

The south wall is the most important because it gets both the morning and afternoon sun. A window-box kitchen garden or breakfast nook should be oriented to the sun. The west wall is the second most important although the east wall gets the breakfast sun.

If you are going to keep the old refrigerator, the way the door opens will restrict its location. Refrigerators and stoves are far-and-away the shoddiest consumer goods on the market so you might give serious thought before installing a planned obsolescence in the heart of your home.

Try out different configurations for a year or so before deciding on your final kitchen; just build shelves and plywood counters with 2×4 frames. Move them around until the placement feels right—when you get the blender off the counter and find a spot for the coffee cone that's convenient you'll have years to enjoy a rare achievement. Try a shelf for the cookbooks and see what it does to your counter lighting. If it isn't right, move it. Your finished cabinetry will be nearly impossible to alter once it's in place.

A completely new kitchen, including wiring, plumbing, new walls and floorcovering, all new cabinets and counters, will take one semi-experienced person with occasional help for the heavy work two to three weeks working full-time. Building the cabinets in advance will cut a week out of the messy part.

The cabinets and trim in this kitchen got a coat of Rez clear sealer before Flecto Salem Maple stain was applied. The stain was applied with a rag and was feathered with a rag dipped in paint thinner. The result of this technique was a good color match between the fir, mahogany and birch. Three coats of satin finish verathane applied with light sandings in between sealed the wood.

These cabinets were constructed to suit the specific pots and pans that the owners had. The shelves slide out on runners so that you don't have to crawl on your hands and knees groveling for the saucepan at the back.

Because there are so many individual steps that don't lend themselves to any sort of organization, a pro can't do it very much faster.

The kitchen on this page cost $1,626.90 in Seattle in 1975 not counting labor or appliances. This total included a new service entry for the electricity—a major portion of the cost of rewiring the house. As modern kitchens require a good deal more electricity than is usually available on the old fusebox, a new service entry is not an uncommon expense in kitchen remodeling. The single drawer unit was custom made by a cabinet shop, as was the frame for the antique windows placed over the sink. The four lead-camed windows were salvaged. The floor is Armstrong Solarium.

Cheaper flooring, homemade drawers and window frame and simpler wiring would have cut the cost of this kitchen by about $500. Leaving the sink in its old location under the new open shelves would have shaved nearly another $100 from the total cost.

These cabinets were owner-built and designed specifically to fit the space available.

The most extravagent expense in this new kitchen was the $193 spent on the new frame for the two lead-camed windows over the sink. Because the sash frames were old, hinges that provide support to the top and bottom horizontal pieces of the frame were used, which required a frame built and routed by a cabinet shop. New sash frames around the glass would have involved less custom work and would have been cheaper. With a new frame a simpler homemade-frame-and-hinge job would have worked.

Splashboard made by 1×4 along the wall at the back of the counter hides the back edge of the formica and protects the wall. White or black silicone bathtub caulk may be used to fill the crack between the formica and the splashboard after the splashboard has been finished.

Tile or formica laid on plywood and trimmed with molding would make alternate higher and lower priced splashboards. Silicone is a good grout for tile in locations that get a lot of traffic because it repels most stains better than plaster grout. Tile will cause grease and moisture to condense and require frequent wiping. Seal the first 3 inches above the splashboard with clear sealer so it will wipe well.

Around cooking and sink areas, the whole wall should be sealed. Clear latex sealer will make matte or semi-gloss paint jobs shinier than the unsealed wall but the change in luster isn't objectionable. The border between sealed and unsealed wall should be as well-hidden as possible.

The counters were set an inch lower than usual at 35 inches in this kitchen to accommodate a short cook, which caused a problem in installing the Kitchen Aide dishwasher. According to the installation instructions, the machine is supposed to fit under a 35-inch counter. But in this case, even with the front adjustment legs removed entirely, the counter trim had to be altered unattractively in order for the door to open. Plumbing a dishwasher is simple, involving a tee in the supply-and-drain lines and a few feet of flexible copper tubing, all of which comes in a kit.

Installation of the Frigidaire drop-in countertop stove was simple following the clear instructions. The formica was snagged and torn during the installation because it came to the very edge of the plywood; it should have stopped back from the edge a fraction. Chrome covers the counter-edge on either side of the stove.

A direct fan, set between the studs over the stove and mounted easily with a saber saw, provides more air circulation with less of an eyesore than more expensive hooded models. The custom-made hood increases the fan's efficiency.

Open shelves involve a trade-off: they are quicker and cheaper to build than closed cabinets, have a light open feeling and show off the fancy crockery. But they don't keep grease from collecting on fancy glasses and serving wine to unexpected guests can lose a lot of its sponteneity when the glasses are thick with grease. Glass doors are an expensive option if you have them made. Doors you make yourself with portable tools are liable to be too rustic to go with the rest of this kitchen. Upper cabinets are the sort of eccentric thing you prowl the salvage yards for and design your kitchen around once you've found them.

The top shelf in these open cabinets has the A-face down as it is seen from below. Shelves rest on 1×2 screwed to the studs. Use the proper counter-sink and do the screwing job right. *It will show!*

The trim in this kitchen is fir. Cabinet sides are A-face shop plywood which has the large-faced grain typical of veneer that's peeled off the log. A fancier sawn face would have been a better choice and would have added only $10 to the cost of the kitchen. Cabinet doors are birch. Vertical grain fir plywood might have been special ordered for about the same price and would have matched the trim.

The woodwork was sanded with 100-grit sandpaper and sealed before staining to avoid blotches. Salem maple stain was chosen for a rich medium tone. It was rubbed on, allowed to settle and rubbed off with paint thinner for a good color match of the mixed woods.

Cabinets with a plywood superstructure are the easiest to build with portable tools and wood-matching skills. If you cut the plywood dividers correctly as a first step—before there are complications and compromises to make—the cabinets will be square when they're finished. This is not always the case with stick-built cabinets where the trim is structural.

Lower kitchen cabinets tend to collect monsters (rarely used utensils, antique olive oil cans, old pot lids). Plywood dividers can't keep the monsters from reproducing, but they do help keep them categorized.

Three-quarter-inch plywood or particle board is even stronger than necessary for kitchen cabinetry but allows ample thickness for dadoes. Three-quarter inch is also the thickness of finished 1-inch trim lumber and this may come in handy for last-minute design changes.

Finished lower cabinets are usually 36-inches high by 24-

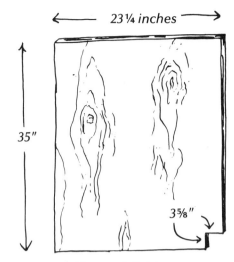

Plywood divider

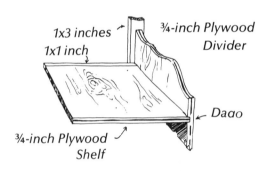

This plywood cabinet is shown from the rear.

Plywood cabinet

inches deep with a 25-inch counter. Plywood dividers should be cut 35 by 23¼ inches to produce this size. Dadoes are cut ¼-inch deep. These dimensions will accommodate most dishwashers.

Lower cabinets are usually raised from the floor to keep them from looking heavy and to provide a space for toes. A cut-out from the lower front corner of the plywood dividers accomplishes this. A cut-out 3⅝ inches square will perfectly fit a 1×4 kickplate leaving no gap for rodents.

The end wall of the cabinets is cut like a divider except that it stops at the bottom of the dado for the bottom shelf. The end of the cabinet rests on a kickplate of 1×4 or 2×4.

One bottom and one middle shelf are all that are required in a cabinet this deep. Dadoes oppose each other wherever two adjoining cabinets have the same shelf arrangement. The ¼ inch of plywood left between the two dadoes is adequate although slightly fragile until the cabinet is fully assembled.

The bottom shelf in plywood frame cabinets is trimmed by the front of the cabinet and is cut the same depth as the dividers. If the doors are recessed, the upper shelves will have to be recessed to allow space. Rip these ¾ inch shallower than the dividers and trim them with 1×1 so the raw edge of plywood doesn't show. The trimmed shelf will be flush with the plywood dividers so that the front trim can be nailed to it.

Square the cabinets as you assemble them with a large framing square and nail diagonals of scrap on the back to keep the cabinet rigid. Remove these just before the cabinets are hung.

Nail-and-glue or clamp-and-glue the façade before nailing the cabinets in place. The horizontal bottom trim runs the full length of the cabinet front. This is usually made of 1×2 nailed flush to the bottom shelf so that the shelf can be easily wiped out. Uprights are of 1×3 between cabinets. The top horizontal piece is broken by the uprights to give them some extra plywood to grab for stability when the doors are working. Wedge-shaped pieces of wood may back the vertical trim at the bottom for extra rigidity. The top horizontal piece is usually 1×2 set flush with the bottom of the counter.

The countertop should be ¾ inch or heavier plywood or particle board. C-face plywood may be used if raised grain is planed down and any gaps are filled with Spackle to give the surface a firm base. Apply the countertop after the cabinets are mounted to the wall. Use flathead screws 1½ inches long properly predrilled so the screw does not damage the plywood endgrain of the divider and sits down flush to the countertop.

Stick built cabinets rely on one or two walls for strength and do not lend themselves to prefabrication, (this lengthens the time that the kitchen is down during a remodeling by as much as a week). The extra one-by stock required usually costs as much as the plywood in divider cabinets. Dadoes aren't necessary, however, which saves a slow careful job.

A frame of 2×4 set 3½ inches in from the façade of the cabinet forms the toe recess. Nail the back 2×4 to the wall and toenail the rest to the floor. Nail the bottom shelf of ¾ plywood or particle board to the 2×4s.

There is no place to hide an error on a flush-mounted door.

This will work better.

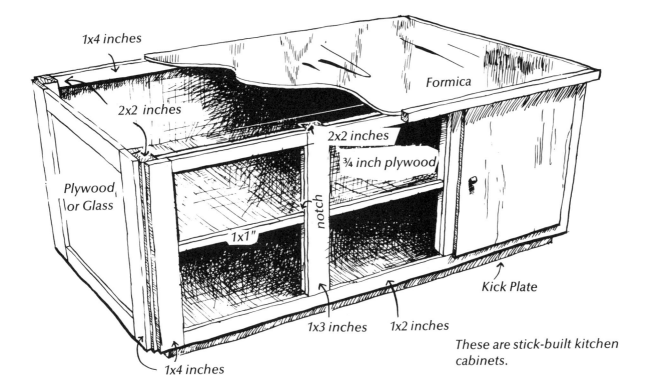

1x4 inches

Formica

2x2 inches

2x2 inches

¾ inch plywood

Plywood or Glass

notch

1x1"

Kick Plate

1x3 inches **1x2 inches**

These are stick-built kitchen cabinets.

1x4 inches

Use 1×2 or 1×4 for framing; 2×4s look clumsy. Nail the supports for the middle shelf and countertop to the wall measuring up from the bottom counter. Don't use a level or you risk building a cabinet out of square which will make the final trimming job nearly impossible.

Use a framing square and true-up as you build the sides of the cabinet. Do not assume the wall is straight or square to either the cabinet or the floor. If you nail strips to the wall to fasten the façade, square the façade to the bottom shelf even if this leaves a widening gap along the wall. If molding won't cover this, custom rip a piece and let molding cover your rough rip.

Cabinet doors are usually recessed into the cabinet to keep them from looking like vaults. To do this the doors are dadoed on all four edges. This job is best done by a table saw, even if you must let it out to a cabinet shop. The dado you make with a hand-held circular saw will not be fine enough to show when the door is opened. You can have the edges routed while you're at the shop and give your cabinets a fancy turn.

Simpler doors can be placed on the outside of the façade of the cabinet. Any irregularity will be less apparent if the edges of the door are cut back at a 45° angle.

Doors set inside the cabinet front flush with the façade should have a border to provide a step-joint or the least irregularity will glare.

The cheap pressed *cabinet hinges* with two screws showing are the easiest to install. Fasten the tongues of two hinges to

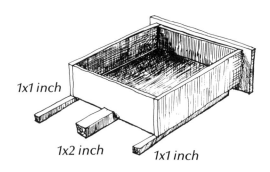

1x1 inch

1x2 inch   1x1 inch

Homemade Guides

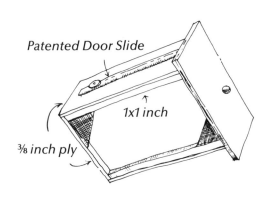

Patented Door Slide

1x1 inch

⅜ inch ply

the back of the door and hold the door in place. The screws to the frame will line up with easy access. These are made to fit either flush, dadoed, or on doors that lie above the cabinet façade.

Hinges which set with both shells hidden are much more difficult to align perfectly. Use wooden toothpicks or pocket-knife slivers and white glue to pad one side of a screw hole that needs slight adjustment. For large adjustments, completely fill the hole with wood slivers and start over. Pieces of matchbook cover stuck under the hinge (accompanied by chanting) can help straighten a door.

Never paint hinges. Paint forms a film when it dries that sticks to itself better than to the metal; it tears when the hinge is flexed. If the hinges were painted before, remove and strip them. A pocketknife does the best job of removing paint from the slot so you can get the screwdriver in it.

If you can afford to let out only one job in remodeling your kitchen, let out the *drawers*. Drawers require precision cutting and a cabinet shop can do a better job for $100-150 a unit, depending on what you order. Be sure to provide stock for the drawer fronts so that the cabinet-shop work will match your own.

A homemade drawer is a simple box of ⅜-inch plywood or ½-inch lumber with a masonite bottom and glued-on front. The bottom may be raised ¾ inch and nailed to 1×1 stringers or it may be set in a dado made by two passes of a circular saw. Tack the side pieces of the drawer to a larger board or work counter. Passes with the saw will be accurate enough if you are very careful. Do your close fitting by rasping away masonite or shimming with slivers of wood.

Two triangles of scrap masonite set in opposing corners will help you square the drawer while the glue is drying.

Don't use contact cement to glue the drawer front onto the box. Contact cement impedes moisture transference and could cause the drawer front to warp. Use white or brown glue.

Adjusting drawers is a tricky job that requires good carpentry and patience. You give up a chance to show some of your carpentry by using patented drawer slides but they do a much easier and more accurate job for about $4 a drawer. Lacquer the drawers inside and out to help assure uniform absorption of moisture.

Setting a sink is not difficult if you resist the temptation to save on plywood. The cutout for the sink ought to come out of the center of a single piece of plywood. Scraps of plywood across the front and back of the sink are cheaper than a single sheet but they add complications at a point where there isn't much room for braces.

The sink requires about ¾ inch around the inside of the cut-out for its fastening devices. This much of the perimeter of the sink can usually be no thicker than 1 inch. See the instructions packed with the individual sink.

Get a double sink; single sinks are only slightly cheaper. Rinsing is done with the water running which is wasteful. A double sink will allow you to stack dirty pots in the sink and still have a clean area for vegetables or getting cooking water.

Self-rimming stainless steel sinks start under $30, usually with the strainer baskets that sit in the drain holes but without faucets. ("Self rimming" means that no separate chrome trim is needed to hide the match between the sink and the countertop. A lip of the sink itself covers the edge of the countertop, riding on a layer of caulk.) Cut-out dimensions are packed with the sink.

The cheapest stainless steel sinks hold up well but are noisy because they amplify the splash of water from the faucet. This noise can be cut down radically by coating the underside of the sink with roofing tar, linoleum adhesive or any other thick goop that does not stay sticky.

The cut-out for the sink is made with a saber saw after the formica is laid. The saber saw will chip the formica but the chips will be covered by the lip of the sink. Do a careful gluing job in this area when you lay the formica.

Upper cabinets here are medicine cabinets from a demolished apartment house. Half-round molding hides the crack between units. Pot-bellied molding trims out the bottom; door-crown molding decorates the top and ties the units together.

Chips missing from heavily painted cabinets can be filled with Spackle. Prime first to assure good adhesion. Sand and prime before you paint to make sure the patch is invisible. The patch is permanent but the cabinet will still be prone to chipping.

The cabinet above the stove is the top half of a carpenter-

The upper cabinets in this kitchen are a combination of medicine cabinets salvaged from an old apartment house and the top half of a freestanding Kitchen Queen.

One-by-two gives the shelves to the right a heavy appearance. Drill before you nail and glue. The kitchen below got oak plywood trimmed with 1x2 oak edges. The doors must be cut on a tablesaw for a perfect glue edge.

built Kitchen Queen, a freestanding top and bottom cabinet unit with counter that was popular before World War I. The lower section with a new countertop and sink is placed in the pantry to the right of the stove where the dishes are washed. The other lower cabinets come from apartment kitchens. Most old drawers run on wooden runners which become sloppy with wear over time. Replace the runners in the cabinet if these are worn, or replace them with drawer hardware which is much easier to adjust (about $4 a drawer).

Rotten double-hung windows were replaced by five transom windows (which originally went over apartment doors for ventilation but are now banned as fire hazards). The fourth window is hinged with a strip of rubber kick molding that happened to be handy. It is tacked from the inside bottom of the top stationary window to the outside top of the one that opens. Butyl rubber caulk lines the crack between rubber and wood.

The kitchen is a favorite spot for wallpaper because it is expensive and kitchens often don't have much open wall to cover. If it isn't the vinyl coated type, a coat of verithane on the paper near the sink will help it wipe clean. The change in luster usually isn't great between sealed and unsealed paper—try a scrap first. The alternative is to lay enough wallpaper aside to recover the sink area at least once during the life of the job.

The drawer unit and the cabinet doors in this kitchen should probably be built by a cabinet shop but the rest of the kitchen can be built with portable tools. With a bit of molding, even the doors could be home built.

Oak is about twice as expensive as clear fir which makes it an option for lightly trimmed open cabinets. Oak usually comes with sharp corners which are easier to use than the rounded corners on clear fir because perpendicular joints don't run into a bevel. Any corner that shows should be rounded by hand sanding after the cabinet is trimmed. Use a block and a rocking motion with 60-grit paper. Polish the job with 100- or 120-grit.

(A pro would use a router to round the edges.) Sharp oak corners on expensive furniture should be taken down by hand.

The sharp corners on milled oak make possible the wood-trimmed formica. A fir 1×2 would have to have one edge taken down by a joiner to meet the edge of the formica without a groove. Use a tung oil finish that can be wiped on the formica and eliminate the need for masking and careful painting.

If scrap formica is used it will probably not come wide enough to cover the long counter and round the corner to reach the sink. A seam in the formica is unsightly no matter how well done. To avoid it, measure the formica you will use and move the sink over or match in a breadboard or marble slab to hide the seam. Or go to more expensive formica. You can use the piece you cut away to cover the other counter space.

The lightwell above the sink was set in the ceiling joists—the joists run parallel to the window so this recess involved only the very quick framing and the extra time spent taping the extra seams in the plasterboard ceiling.

The upper open cabinets are ¾-inch plywood. The shelves, including the bottom shelf, sit in dadoes in the upright sides. The top shelf is dadoed to hold the uprights tying the unit together. One-by-twos screwed to the wall studs and the cabinet run above the top shelf and under the bottom.

Three-quarter inch plywood or particle board shelves up to 12 inches deep can span 4 feet. Longer shelves will need support along the wall, at least in the middle. Usually a full length strip of 1×2 is used for appearance. Shelves deeper than 12 inches and longer than 4 feet will need front support as well.

Upper cabinets with doors are built in the same manner. If the doors are to be inset, the inner shelves must be recessed.

Formica is one of the few space-age products to have earned its place in old houses; it is simply superior to everything else. It cleans up better and stays new looking longer than any other surface except tile which is *much* more expensive. Laying formica isn't difficult but it is scary. Formica is extremely hard but is also brittle and you must be careful from the time you buy it until it is finally laid. Scrap sheets 3 by 10 feet can usually be found in salvage and discount centers in a good range of colors for under $20. Because paint comes in an even wider variety of colors, it's a good idea to pick your formica and floor covering first.

The sheet is rolled for transport and taped. Compressing the roll or allowing it to spring open when the tape is cut will break it into useless scrap.

Unroll the sheet carefully on a hard floor (not carpet) and accurately measure and mark your cuts. As excess will have to be taken away by hand with a file, accuracy is more important here than in most jobs that you will do yourself.

Cut 1/16-inch oversize on lead edges so that you can make it fit perfectly with a file. Cut a good ¼-inch undersize at walls so that any pounding between the counter and the wall doesn't

Align the formica at the lead edge so that it will go down straight. Then remove the newspaper and lay the formica down, being careful not to catch air bubbles under it.

Apply the formica to the edges of the counter first; then file it flush to the plywood.

¾-inch plywood of C-grade or better.

touch the formica. A 1×4 splash plate covered with formica or finished with wood runs along the wall on top of the counter, giving you ¾ inch to hide the back of the formica and any unevenness in the wall.

The plywood countertop shouldn't have any gaps or skips that might allow the formica to break if a sharp blow hits it. If your sheet has flaws over ¼-inch wide, fill them with Spackle or floor-leveling compound.

As formica will not stick permanently to a plywood edge, the plywood must be trimmed with wood. One-by-one will do the job but gives a very flimsy looking counter which is usually unsatisfactory. One-by-two is standard counter-edge trim.

Formica is cut with a special carbide-tipped knife. The hard colored surface is carefully scratched until the knife penetrates to the softer brown layer underneath. Once the blade has a track to follow, bear down hard and cut most of the way through the brown underlayer. The sheet will snap neatly in two. Use a metal straightedge or framing square to guide your knife on the initial passes.

Give the counter edge two coats of contact cement. The first coat is absorbed by the wood. A single coat will do on the formica. Allow the cement to sit until it is dry to the touch.

Apply the edge formica to the sides of the counter first, allowing it to project above the top of the plywood just enough to clean up nicely with a file. The two surfaces coated with dry contact cement will bond instantly so line the formica up carefully along the top before touching it to the wood.

File the corners smooth so that the front piece can lay over them smoothly. This joint will show. File it as well.

When formica has been laid on all edges of the counter, file it flush with the countertop, holding the file parallel with the top and cutting only on the push stroke. Lift the file on back strokes to avoid damaging the teeth or chipping the formica. Some scratches in the countertop plywood are inevitable and benign, but don't chew it up unnecessarily and don't put dips in it. If you've made a flaw in the filing, leave it. You can't dig your way out of a hole. A pro would do this job with a router. Doing it by hand takes about an hour for a 10-foot counter.

When the edges are filed, give the plywood top two coats of contact cement and give the back of the formica one coat. Allow these to dry completely. Any moist spots will cause problems in the next step.

Because the formica can't be shifted once it has touched the cemented plywood, lining it up requires a trick. Cover the dry plywood with a single layer of newspaper (except for the ¼ inch closest to you) and slide the formica around until it is positioned exactly. Press down along the lead edge to get good adhesion. Lift the back of the formica, remove the newspaper, and press the formica down to the plywood. Work the area making contact back from front to back to assure that you don't catch air underneath.

Finish off the perimeter of the counter with a file as you did the edge formica.

Wood edged counters are attractive and less work. Apply the formica and file it to a sharp 90° before you apply the 2×2 edge trim. Pay a shop a dollar or two to plane one edge of the 1×2 flat so that its corners are no longer rounded. If you leave the round in, it will catch crumbs and make the counter hard to wipe off. Dowels make a fine trim detail fastening the counter edge in place. Oak trim doesn't have rounded corners and saves the planing.

Where the counter turns there will be a joint in the formica. Clean both edges as neatly as you can with a file before you lay the formica and either live with the seam that results or design around it. The most logical breaks in the countertop that can be used to hide necessary seams are the stove and the sink. Less obvious breaks would be an inset slab of marble for rolling dough or an inset cutting board.

A slab of marble can be glued to the plywood counter or set below it on a second piece of plywood. Cutting boards should not be nailed down. You lose the use of the second surface and the board may warp from uneven moisture. Large cutting boards are readily available and not expensive to have made by a shop with a planer. Insist that the grain be alternated on the boards that go into it so it won't curl.

Plumbing is a miserable job. If you can possibly leave the sink in its old location, or near enough to it to reach from the old plumbing coming out of the wall, do so. Assembling plumbing properly is not especially difficult but there is rarely room to work. Stirring up the old plumbing is risky. Halfway through a kitchen is a poor time to discover that you have to stop and replumb the house.

Three types of plumbing are in common use: galvanized steel pipe which must be threaded and which most old houses have; rigid-copper which solders together with heat; and PVC (plastic pipe) which is glued together. PVC is usually used for drains.

In galvy or copper, ½-inch pipe is used to supply the kitchen and bath; ¾ inch for the house intake from the water source. Two-inch galvy or plastic pipe is used for all drains.

If you decide to move the sink, move the plumbing before you set the cabinets so you work with access to the wall.

Start at a threaded end on the old galvanized pipe or rent a pipe cutter and a threader from a rental shop to make your own threaded end. Galvy can be cut with a hacksaw but a pipe

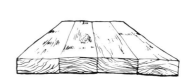

The grain of the pieces of wood used to make a breadboard should alternate so that the board won't warp.

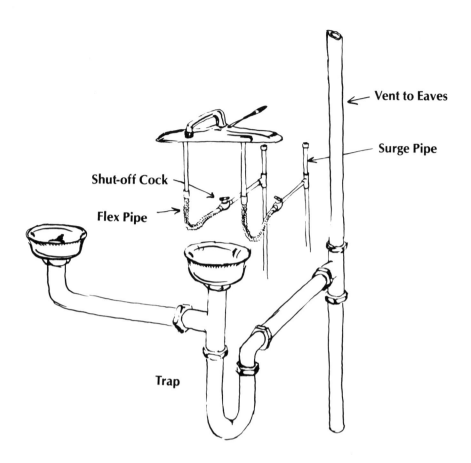

Vent to Eaves

Surge Pipe

Shut-off Cock

Flex Pipe

Trap

cutter does an easier job. A pipe cutter consists of a sharp hardened steel wheel that is held against the pipe by a pair of rollers opposite. As the cutter is revolved around the pipe, the wheel etches a line. Tightening the cutter forces the line deeper on subsequent revolutions until the line neatly severs the pipe.

A pipe threader fits on the end of the pipe and is revolved. The first teeth of the threader cut light spirals. Subsequent teeth deepen these to a finished threaded end. Plenty of cutting oil is necessary for the job. The cutter and threader are easy to understand once you have them in your hand. A day's rental on the two is about $8.

New hot and cold water pipes can be installed in galvy or rigid-copper. If you can reuse the old galvy fittings, galvy may be cheaper. If you must go to all new materials, rigid-copper will be cheaper because galvy elbows and tees are expensive and the bends and twists required to get the water to the sink require many of these.

To install galvy, map your route carefully on paper, figuring the length of each cut piece of pipe. There is very little room to cheat with galvy. Turns must be an honest 45° or 90°. Putting pressure on the pipe to line up a bad fit will result in leaks. Add 1 inch to each pipe to allow for the amount that will be threaded into the fittings (½ inch at each end) and subtract the length of the fitting itself. As this varies, you'll have to measure the elbows and tees you will actually use. The plumbing shop can custom cut and thread pipe about as cheaply as you can do the

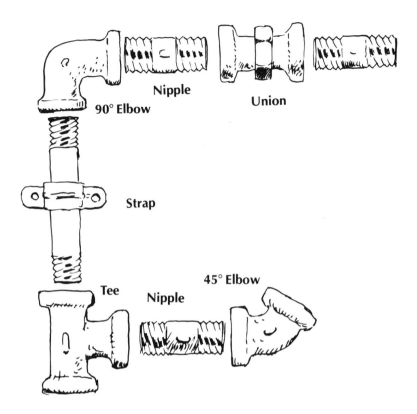

90° Elbow   **Nipple**   **Union**

Strap

Tee   **Nipple**   **45° Elbow**

job yourself with rental tools and carries many lengths in stock already threaded.

Apply pipe-joint compound to the threads and assemble; it helps keep the joints from leaking and keeps them from freezing together so they can be disassembled later. Two pipe wrenches are required, working in opposite directions to twist a pipe and a fitting together or apart.

Because plumbing is all threaded the same way, it cannot be disassembled from the middle. You must start at one end. Unions solve this problem. Saw any pipe in two, back out the two halves with pipe wrenches and shorten one of them by the length of the union you are using. Thread both ends of the pipe you cut and apply the union. There is usually enough swing in the plumbing to move the cut pipe apart for backing it out. If there isn't, cut the pipe twice to give yourself room to work. When swinging plumbing around that you want to keep, move it so that the joint is loosened. It will then retighten when you swing the pipe back into place.

The union consists of three pieces. An end threads onto each end of pipe. A third piece joins these two.

All plumbing must be strapped in place so that it won't vibrate and develop leaks. If you use bent nails for straps, pad the pipe with a scrap of leather or wadded newspaper so the nail won't wear a hole in the pipe. Special straps cost about 15¢ and do a much better job.

Use rigid-copper unless you have a lot of salvage galvy

around. It goes together easier and can be joined to galvy with a special connector.

Rigid-copper is cut with a pipe cutter identical to that used for galvy but smaller. As the cuts are not threaded or cleaned up in any way, a hacksaw cut is unsatisfactory. The least burr or distortion will ruin the joint.

Pipe cutters for rigid-copper can be bought from the sale tool bin at most hardware stores (find one with a metal body). The plastic-bodied models are not stable enough to make a consistent cut. A good cutter costs under $8 and will accept ½- and ¾-inch pipe.

Rigid-copper fittings are simple cylinders and tees with an inside diameter that precisely matches the outside diameter of the pipe. The pipe is inserted ½ inch into the fitting and soldered. A shoulder inside the fitting sets the depth of the insertion so it's difficult to go wrong.

After cutting the pipe to length, trial-assemble the unit to see that you have it right. Polish the end of the pipe and the inside of the fitting with steel wool and paint both with liquid flux solder made for rigid-copper. Assemble the pieces that join at any one connector and solder them all at once.

Heat is applied with a butane torch. To light it, turn the gas on to prime the nozzle with gas, then turn it off. Slowly turn it back on with a match held in front of it. Too much gas will blow out the match, so it takes practice. Allow the nozzle to heat up a full minute before turning the torch upside down to work.

The flux solder dries a dull grey after you paint it on. When it bubbles out of the joint a bright liquid silver, remove the heat and allow it to cool.

Heat the joint at one spot with the torch until the solder first bubbles, then slowly revolve the torch around the joint until the melting is complete. Heat the joint fast enough to finish before enough heat is transferred across the fitting to melt the previous joint.

Melting all the solder out of a joint will cause a leak.

Rigid-copper unions are so cheap that the best way to repair a bad joint is to cut both or all three pipes back 6 inches or so, apply unions and new pipe, and start over.

You can sometimes repair a leak by painting solder on the outside and heating the joint until the solder melts and is sucked into the crack. Usually this takes so long that you melt the other joints on the fitting but it is worth a try. A wet rag wrapped around the joints you don't want to melt helps a little.

Fittings for rigid-copper are made of rolled copper like the pipe itself or are cast. The prices of the two types are competitive. The cast fittings transfer heat more slowly from the joint you are working to the joint that you don't want to melt and may be easier to use.

When soldering cast copper turn-offs in place, be sure to disassemble the cock and remove the stem and rubber components or you may damage them. Cocks are also available to thread onto male or female fittings soldered in place.

To get from the existing galvy to new rigid-copper plumbing, start with a male or female threaded fitting on the copper. This may be threaded onto the old pipe direct or through a union. If you thread it direct, do so before you put the rest of the copper assembly together so you can turn the fitting.

The lightweight plumbing between the wall and the sink is built with compression fittings. These vary in detail but all use a rubber washer which is compressed by some sort of cap to make a watertight seal.

Drain connections are cut to length with a hacksaw, filed clean and slipped together. As long as no obstruction prevents alignment of the connection between the trap and the heavy 2-inch drain stand, assembly is easy. You may have to turn the heavy pipe to get it aligned so some access for a pipewrench should be left. It won't have to be altered once it's right for the sink, so the wall can be sealed afterward.

Intake lines can be more difficult because water pressure is greater. A leak means the joint has pressure on it throwing it to one side. Bend the flex pipe over its whole length until joints line up.

Heavy string pulled through the melted candle wax will make a workable compression washer if you don't have one the right size for a replacement. Assortment packages are cheap.

Intake lines should have surge pipes plumbed onto them. Use a tee instead of an elbow before the line comes out of the wall and run up a foot or so to a cap. The trapped air works as a shock absorber. If water surge comes back later on making your lines clunk drain the system to refill the surge pipes with air.

The ¾-inch water intake line bringing water into the house usually divides at the water heater. Separate ½ inch lines hot and cold can run from here directly to the bathroom and cut down on loss of water pressure if someone flushes a toilet elsewhere while you're in the shower. This is called "double plumbing."

Kitchen floors are usually in the worst shape of any part of an old house. If there isn't any money but the current floor is shot, try refinishing the wood floor under the old linoleum. A butane torch and a stiff putty knife will remove the old linoleum and most of the thick black mastic. Finish as you would any other wood floor and figure on renewing the finish yearly.

Linoleum isn't made in this country any more. Everything called linoleum is vinyl. Vinyl squares should be started from a chalkline in the middle of the room because walls are unreliable straight lines and a crooked start involves either taking up what you have done and starting over or doing complicated razor-knife work trying to get it straight. Work from the middle out to the walls and fit complicated pieces before applying the mastic.

Squares are available adhesive backed with peel-off paper. These are a convenience of the ignorant. Linoleum paste spreads easily and quickly with a toothed spreader. The distance between teeth regulates the application. The store selling the vinyl usually sells mastic and can tell you which trowel

Linoleum Knife

to buy. Latex linoleum paste has no odor and cleans up quickly with a wet rag before drying. If you allow gobs of it to dry before you lay vinyl on them, you will have to scrape it away.

Both squares and sheet vinyl should be left in the house overnight at 70° so they are soft and will lie flat and cut easily.

Apply mastic to a small area of floor at a time 1 to 2 inches beyond the tiles you'll lay so that the next mastic won't have to be worked close to the last round of squares laid. At doors and other obstructions, custom cut tile-by-tile with a linoleum knife. Stiff paper templates cut out so much faster than flooring that they save time.

Clean up all seams with a rag and water before the mastic turns clear. A bit of sink cleanser speeds the job but don't rub or you'll damage the surface of the tiles.

The subfloor under the vinyl must be perfect because the least ridge or crevice will translate to the new flooring. If the old floor is linoleum that is still in fair shape, nail down any high corners or loose seams with roofing nails which have a very thin sharp-edged head. Level any cracks or missing sections with floor-patching compound. Plane and sand flat before laying the new vinyl.

If the old floor is in poor condition, lay a subfloor of particle board. Pressed board wall panelling ¼ inch thick and used upside-down works well and is cheap. Fill missing areas with patching compound before laying the subflooring. Taper changes in level over the longest possible distance. A broad-knife works well for this. If the floor is very rough, use ½- or ⅝-inch particle board. Nail the subflooring 1 inch in from the edge every 6 inches or so. Nail your way down the sheet from one end to assure the board goes down flat. Patch any missing chips or cracks large enough to accept compound. If there is any question whether an area needs filling, pass mud over it and scrape it away. This very quick operation will assure a lasting job. Particle board doesn't usually dimple with the last blow of the hammer to set the nail but a quick pass of mud will double check and point out any nails that stick up.

Sheet vinyl is harder to lay but your first try will turn out well if you are careful in your cutting. Whenever possible push the vinyl itself up to the wall to mark it for cutting rather than using measurements. Mistakes are expensive. Small patches don't lay well. A rounded inside corner is less likely to tear than are two sharp crossed lines. Cut and fit until the sheet fits within one-half inch of the wall everywhere that will be covered by quarter-round. It must fit perfectly where it will show.

If two or more sheets are needed, they must overlap so that the pattern lines up perfectly. Fit the more complicated piece first. Rough cut the second piece, align it perfectly with the first and recut to fit.

Glue both pieces down except the area 2 or 3 inches on either side of the seam you will cut. Inside doorways and along walls where the cut of the vinyl must fit perfectly because it will not be covered by trim, cut and bully the vinyl down with a block of wood or screwdriver. *Cut—push—recut* works better than measurements.

Cut both sheets at one time with the linoleum knife while they are overlapped. Lift the edges enough to smear mastic on the subfloor and rub the seam down with the handle of the linoleum knife. The seam should nearly disappear. Spot gluing in doorways and in corners and along seams is enough unless the vinyl wants to lift.

Adding a window garden to a southern or western wall will allow you to grow chives, lettuce, tomatoes and other produce. Grow-lux lamps at the top will extend the growing season to most of the year. The spot lamps work better at long distances than the tubes.

Window gardens are simple to design. Use ¾-inch plywood on the sides and you will have sufficient width to nail directly to the frame of the window. Plywood has enough shear strength to eliminate the need for bracing unless the extension is 30 inches or deeper. The sash windows removed from the frame can be tacked to the outside of the extension, requiring new glass only on the sides. If you don't put glass on the sides, use mirror tiles to make the most of the light that enters through the front.

The simple box drawn here has plywood sides over 2×4 and 2×3 framing. The plywood is cut out on the sides slightly larger than the opening between the two-bys to form a ledge for the side windows. Float a ¾- by ¾-inch wood strip over the glass and nail it diagonally into the studs. Nails into the edge of the plywood won't hold. Drill first to make the nailing easier.

Salvaged sash windows were nailed to the outside of the frame of this extended windowbox. Caulk protected from the sun by wooden batts serves to separate the windows. The tops are tucked high under the eaves to eliminate flashing problems. The weight of the roof is borne by headers on posts at the top of the filon skylight.

CATALOG OF GREAT STUFF TO SEND AWAY FOR

Old house renovation has gotten past the fad stage and now supports the small companies that furnish supplies that might have folded a few years ago. Moldings in particular are becoming easier to find as production millwork shops get orders and add blades to their inventories. Often your best source of moldings is the nearest city. If you don't have a production milling shop nearby, several are listed here that will ship small quantities to you. The list is basic enough to offer most of the kinds of things you might need.

Molding is run through a machine called a "sticker." If you are looking for custom milling, ask whether the shop has one of these. Four blades shape the four edges. Two edges are usually left black or are given a simple step and can use the blades they have on hand. Custom millings made to order will require grinding two new blades, which will usually add about $50 to the cost of your run regardless of how much stock you order.

Plumbing hardware has been slighted in this catalog because most of it is so incredibly expensive. Ingenuity is the best answer to your fixture needs. You can find an old toilet that has a pipe between the tank and the bowl and build your own wall-mounted toilet for a quarter of the cost of a new reproduction. Drill a hole in the handle and add a chain.

You are usually better off replacing the workings inside the tank rather than trying to repair the workings if they are faulty. If you want an oak tank, have the copper liner constructed to your specifications and build the oak box yourself. You'll save the 100 percent markup at the retail outlet. The companies making reproduction toilets are so small

that they can't build the tank for much less than you can.

Oak seats and accessories are the sort of thing that you can buy from your local craftsmen. Get them at a street fair and you'll strike a blow against the 9 to 5 job.

Salvaged faucets are cheaper than new even if you put some money into them. A radiator shop can boil them out if they are scaly from mineral-laden water. A plating shop that specializes in auto bumpers can either re-plate them in chrome or polish the brass. (Try the Yellow Pages under "Acme.")

New rubber washers will fix most old faucets unless the threads are gone. Even if the threads or washer seat must be re-machined—in addition to boiling and re-plating—the finished fixture will often be cheaper than a new one.

Porcelain and enamelled iron sinks and tubs are best gotten from salvage yards that specialize in house demolition. Plumbing shops often keep old fixtures when they replace them with new and are also a good source. Try to arrive at a time when the shop isn't busy and you may get all the parts you need for the repair and the installation in one shop.

Superficial scratches, dull spots and some stains will come out of porcelain or enamel with rubbing compound from an auto supply store and 600-grit wet and dry sandpaper. Chips look better left as they are than they do painted.

Marble is porous and stains deeply. If the piece looks dowdy when you find it, there isn't much you can do to improve it. Holes for the sink and fittings can be cut at home with a masonry bit but a cemetary marker company is set up to do the job and the cost of the cutting and drilling is usually less than you stand to lose by

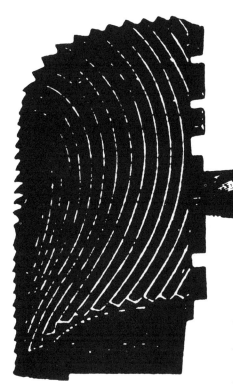

tomers is given here to offer an idea of what is available and what it costs. The range of hardware available is nearly as large as it has ever been. Ask these companies for their catalogs which they'll be happy to send you for free or at a small cost.

breaking the piece trying to do it yourself.

Marble-topped washstands are still fairly cheap in antique stores because they aren't big enough to make a good sideboard. If you have a marble shop cut the hole for the sink, you can convert it into a plumbed vanity. Get a stand that isn't veneer and install a fan in the cabinet to cut down on steam damage. Strip off the old varnish, which will turn soft in steam, and seal the piece inside and out with plastic resin.

Any key shop will replace a missing key if you take the lock out of the door or drawer and take it in. Often a stock key bought right off the rack for under $2 will do the job with no special work. Fancier locks will require a custom key but this is still usually less than $5. After watching the man easily make a key directly from the lock, you'll never feel safe in your locked house again.

A sampling of hardware from a couple of the larger companies that will deal directly with cus-

Stencil

Design rollers and graining tools are available from the Stencil Specialty and stamp either latex or oil-based paint onto the wall or woodwork in the pattern that you choose. The design rollers are available with fill-type tanks or with a foam roller that is first filled with paint in a pan and then thinned to the right density on a newspaper before the print is struck. Paint the wall and allow it to dry. Then strike a guideline with a chalk line and roll the design on from top to bottom. The rubber stamp will fill the void areas with irregular shapes. Complete instructions are included. Send a check with your order; freight is collected COD. The minimum order at this time is $25 for the supplies that run from $4 for the graining roller set, to a design roller with an A-frame and a sponge roller for $16. Write to them to see all the patterns available: *Stencil Specialty Company, 377 Ocean Avenue, Jersey City, NJ 07305.*

Megan Parry

Megan Parry has over fifty stencil designs on hand that they call Early American or Victorian. Many borders work either vertically or horizontally and you should specify which you need when ordering. Custom sizes are available but add $5 per design. Custom designs will be made into stencils from your photos, clippings or sketches for about $25 each. Instructions, supplies' list, and postage are included in the price of the stencils, which run between $20 and $30 and vary in dimension between 4 and 8½ inches. Send for a sample sheet. *Megan Parry, 1727 Spruce, Boulder, CO 80302.*

Focal Point

The molded polymer in these decorations has the approximate density of white pine; it can be sanded, nailed or screwed. Normal installation is done with mas-

tic and the moldings are only suitable for exterior use if they are kept well painted. When figuring the length you'll need add an extra foot per corner for a good pattern match. The moldings are shipped in 10 foot sections—the minimum order is 40 feet. Order one tube of mastic for each 100 feet of molding (a tube costs $4). The moldings will come primed white unless you specify beige for dry-brush staining. Number 100 shown here has inside and outside corners available at $10.30 and $14.30 respectively. The design repeats itself every 10½ inches. Number 104 has inside corners only (at $11) and repeats every 3½ inches. Installation instructions come with your order and you can buy samples for $1.75, which includes shipping. Patterns can be mixed for a quantity price break.

The molded polymer rosettes are applied with mastic as the plaster rosettes are. Polymer rosettes are suitable for use outside only if they are kept well-

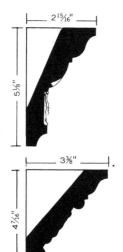

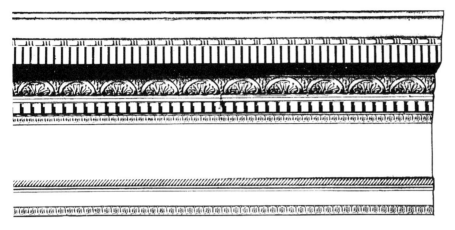

painted or are shaded from the sun. Ceiling medallion number 803 is 24 inches in diameter and costs about $67.

The prices quoted in the catalog are all FOB, Marietta, Georgia. Georgia residents must pay sales tax and there is a $5 handling charge on orders under $100. No returns are permitted without permission. Canadian residents must pay 10 percent extra unless you're remitting on a bank in the U.S. Send your payment with the order; freight can be paid collect. Allow three to four weeks for delivery. *Focal Point, Inc., 4870 South Atlanta Road, Smyrna, GA 30080.*

Driwood

These moldings are milled of kiln-dried poplar, unsanded for painting purposes (but quotations are available on other hardwoods). The decoration is milled and embossed, in some cases, with a build-up of wood fibers. Radii and curves are available. Assemblies are shipped in pieces; furring strips may be needed for the assembly and the placement of cornices. Pieces are shipped in random lengths from 4 to 6 feet long. You can specify the lengths you need but they will cost more. These goods will take a stain-and-oil finish.

The ceiling cornices run from $1.35 per lineal foot to $5.86 for an assembly that includes furring. The chair rails, and door and window casings run from 86 cents through $1.50. The moldings run from 51 cents through $1.35. Plate rails and ceiling panels are also available. The shipping is usually done by truck within two weeks of the receipt of your order. Prior permission is required for returns, with a 10 percent handling charged. There are free samples available that can be ordered from their $1 catalog. A 50 percent deposit is required on COD orders and a $5 minimum packing fee is charged on orders under $25. *Driwood Ornamental Wood Moulding & Millwork, P.O. Box 1729, Florence, SC 29503.*

Allied Design

Allied Design Services makes plaster of Paris brackets rosettes cast from molds made from the originals. They offer eight different bracket designs ranging in price from $10 to $23, and twelve different rosettes ranging in size from 3½ to 30 inches and in price from $6.50 to $60. COD orders will be accepted but you should call or write first to arrange shipping. *Peter and Helene Marchant, Allied Design Services, 1200 Sacramento Street, San Francisco, CA 94108, (415) 673-5723.*

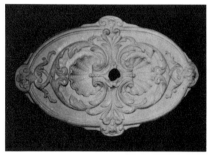

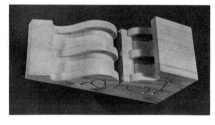

Visallobee's

These plaster appliques are from molds made from the original San Francisco pieces. Visallobee's will ship COD with a 20 percent deposit. California residents should add 6 percent sales tax and freight and packing varies with the size of the order. Diana is 10 by 4 by 9 inches and costs $13. The cupid is 12 by 5 by 10 inches and costs $14. The angel is 7 by 5 by 7 inches and costs $10; the wood corbel is 6¼ by 5¼ by 13½ inches and costs $27.50. The rosettes range in price from $16 to $60 and measure from 11 to 30 inches in diameter. Write to *Visallobee's, 33 Bartlett Street, San Francisco, CA 94110.*

Preservation

Bronze and brass castings made by the *cire-perdu* (or lost wax) process are available from the Preservation Resource Center. Reproductions are 2 to 3 percent smaller and may vary slightly in color from the original due to differences in modern-day alloys. Wrought ironwork is reproduced in bronze with a black patina that is "virtually foolproof to the eye." Prices vary considerably. A Victorian window lift cast in one piece (the originals were in two pieces) will cost approximately $20 for the mold and $3 to $5 for each copy made. For an estimate, ship a sample of the piece to be reproduced, with $2 for its handling and return. Enclose a self-addressed label. The original will be returned with the estimate.

Preservation's simple moldings are suitable for use as door and window casings, chair rails, and baseboards (though single piece baseboards offer less flexibility for hiding irregularities in the wall than a molding placed on top of a board). One is available in ⅜ inch thickness for use over wallboard that has been placed over the old wall. These millings are based on original work by carpenters using hand planes and are authentic to the Federal period. They are included here because the price is so attractive.

The prices quoted by the company are for standard air-dried stock with small natural and milling flaws. If you want the work flawless and sanded add 120 percent to the cost. If the work is to be finished add 80 percent for standard stock sanded. The minimum order is 24 feet and will be shipped in 8-foot lengths. Short lengths of from 3 to 4 feet are available at a 20 percent discount. You can get 4-inch samples for $2 each which includes postage. Custom work will be done from your own sample or drawing at a lineal-foot rate plus knife charge. The prices of the standard patterns run from 30 through 80 cents per lineal foot. New York residents must add 7 percent tax. Your payment is required with the order and you should allow 30 days for delivery by truck. *Preservation Resource Center, Lake Shore Road, Essex, NY 12936.*

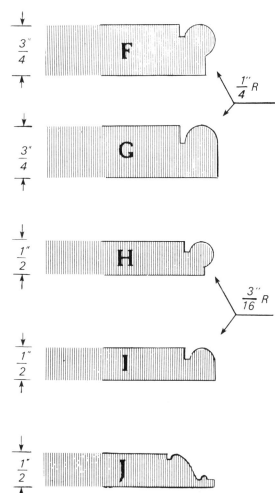

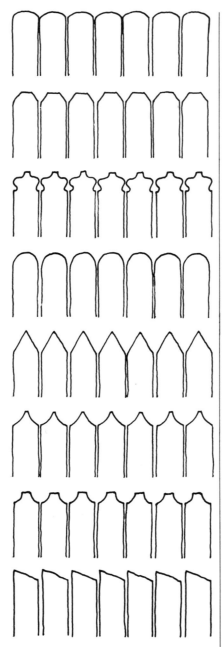

Shingles

Fancy-butt red cedar shingles—such as these varieties: diagonal, half-cove, diamond, round, acorn, octagonal, arrow, and fish scale—are available in your own area. You can get information concerning local distributors from *Red Cedar Shingle and Handsplit Shake Bureau, 5510 White Building, Seattle, WA 98101.*

Horton Brasses

Victorian hardware and black iron knockers are available from Horton Brasses, which makes copies in the same manner that the originals were made. The brasses come with either an "antique" or "bright" finish, designated in the catalog as "A" or "B." You can also get a semi-bright finish at no extra charge. The drawer pulls and keyholes range in price from 65 cents apiece to $3.75, for a fancy pull in the golden oak style. They even have stamped brass back plates "with Wood Tear Drops painted black as the old ones were."

The knockers are forged iron with smooth black-painted finishes and pyramid-head wood screws. The minimum order is $7.50 plus 15 percent to cover first-class postage (the excess postage is refunded). Include payment with your order. Canadians are asked to remit in U.S. funds. Connecticut residents must add 7 percent sales tax. A charge of 15 percent is levied against returns. Send $1.25 for a catalog to *Horton Brasses, P.O. Box 95, Nooks Hill Road, Cromwell, CT 06416.*

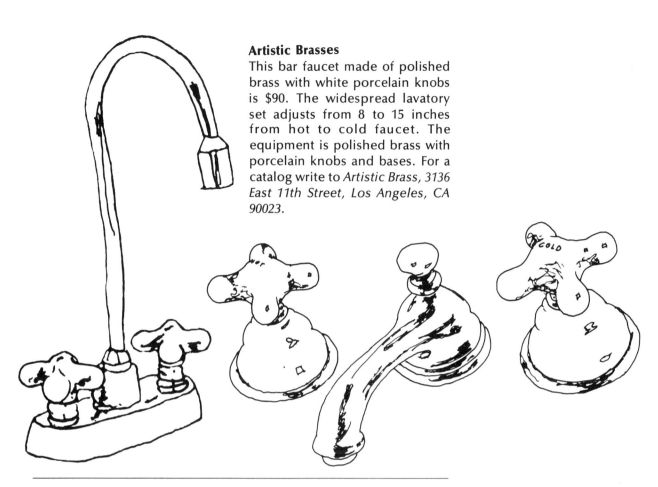

Artistic Brasses
This bar faucet made of polished brass with white porcelain knobs is $90. The widespread lavatory set adjusts from 8 to 15 inches from hot to cold faucet. The equipment is polished brass with porcelain knobs and bases. For a catalog write to *Artistic Brass, 3136 East 11th Street, Los Angeles, CA 90023.*

Heads Up
This wall-mounted oak pull-chain toilet retails for $480 without the seat. The oak seat is available with a stained or natural finish and either chrome or brass fittings for $65. The shipping weight is 8 pounds. Send your payment with the order (unless you have a credit rating with Dun & Bradstreet). If you don't like what you get, you must have the supplier authorize your return. The discounts are substantial if you can find someone with a store to order for you wholesale. California residents should add 6 percent sales tax. *Heads Up, Inc., 3201 West MacArthur Blvd., Santa Ana, CA 92704.*

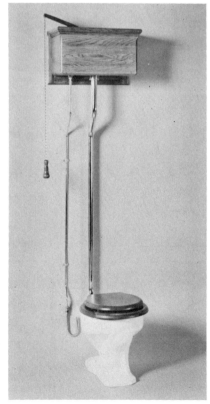

Hallelujah

New redwood appliques, porch brackets and moldings are milled from dried redwood of paint-grade or better by Hallelujah. This shop will also quote on custom work to be done from your photos or drawings. Samples cost 50 cents per pattern. Shipping on the moldings is done in 6 to 14 foot random lengths.

All the millings may vary slightly in size from estimates because of variations in the milling process. The appliques and brackets are manufactured with waterproof glue and galvanized fasteners. The appliques shown here vary in dimension from 4 to 8 inches across; all are 1 inch deep. This porch bracket measures 13 inches in length and width and costs $14. The smaller one measures 9 by 9 inches and costs $3. Porch railing and repeating ornaments are available in a variety of patterns such as those shown here; both railing designs come in pairs selling for $5.50.

Corbels and incised panels come in a variety of designs and dimensions, including the ones shown here. This corbel is $16 and measures 7 by 16 by 3 inches. The panels are 8 inches square and cost about $4. Send $1 for an illustrated catalog, shipping included. Terms include COD or payment with your order. Returns of the millings are accepted within ten days of purchase. Allow two to three weeks for delivery. California residents should add 6 percent sales tax. *Hallelujah Redwood Products, 39500 Comptche Road, Mendocino, CA 95460.*

Kenneth Lynch

At the turn of the century two dozen companies—some with as many as a hundred employees—engaged in the manufacture of stamped zinc ornaments. Today, as far as Kenneth Lynch knows, his is the only company in the country that is still stamping zinc with the old dies. He has ten thousand patterns and his catalog is a joy to be had for $2.50.

The ornaments include brackets, drops and pinnacles, conductor heads, shields, garlands, moldings, top scrolls, leaves and rosettes that vary in price from 90 cents a foot for a thin molding to $83 for a fancy garland done in zinc. Copper ornaments can be made from the same dies but the price fluctuates with the current price of copper. The stampings are furnished to you unassembled; packing containers and freight are extra. "If someone is purchasing just a few ornaments to restore a house we will certainly take care of it," they say, "but there will be a $25 charge for this service." *Kenneth Lynch & Sons, 78 Danbury Road, Wilton, CT 06897.*

Cumberland

Cumberland Woodcraft products, including the brackets, corbels and ceiling drops seen here, are shipped already sanded and assembled. The grilles are made of ¾-inch kiln-dried oak with 1⅛ inch by ¾ inch frames. Beading and dowels are made of hardwood, usually maple or beech. The standard lengths for these ceiling drops are 4, 5 and 6 feet, but custom lengths and depths are also available.

The CB corbel series is made of solid poplar, and is shipped without the crown molding. The corbels are suitable for either exterior or interior use. The brackets are made of solid oak with ¾ inch by 1⅛ inch frames and ¾ inch fretwork. There is a 5 percent charge for crating that is reduced slightly for multiple orders. *Cumberland Woodcraft Company, Walnut Bottom Road, Box 452, Carlisle, PA 17013.*

GLOSSARY

Annular Rings. The growth rings of a tree that form the grain of sawn lumber.

Balloon Framing. The most common type of house construction in the United States. The walls bear the weight of the upper stories and the roof, as opposed to post-and-beam construction in which the walls are suspended curtains that bear no weight.

Balustrade. The row of posts, often decorative, that supports a handrail on a porch or stairway. Commonly called a *banister*.

Bastard File. A medium-grade file used on laminates and plastics. Finer toothed files are used to remove metal; coarser files, called *rasps* are used on wood.

Batt. A thin strip of wood used to cover a seam, as to protect tar from the sun on a roof or to cover the joint between upright boards as in board and batt exterior walls.

Board Foot. The standard measurement of lumber, equal to 1 square foot 1 inch thick. Quantity lumber is quoted in dollars per thousand board feet. This price determines the retail price which is usually expressed in *lineal feet*. One lineal foot (LF) of 1×3 = ¼ board foot (BF).

Bearing Walls. A wall in a balloon framed house which supports the upper stories or roof. Bearing walls run perpendicular to the floor or ceiling joists above and care must be taken when disrupting them.

Boats. Patches in the face of C-grade plywood, so called because their shape resembles a fat canoe. Boats will show through a coat of paint unless the wood is primed and Spackled.

Bull Nose Stop. A milling measuring ½ inch by a little over 1 inch with one rounded edge, milled for use as parting bead in double-hung windows but is commonly used for trim.

Chair Rail. A decorated rail of wood and molding set about 3 feet above floor level to protect walls from the backs of chairs in Victorian houses.

Chuck. The clamping apparatus on a drill which holds the drill bit. Also the two revolving ends on a lathe which hold the wood stock to be turned.

Corner Bead. Aluminum strips nailed over wallboard to form a ridge or bead along the corner to guide the broadknife.

Countersink. A special bit that drills a conical depression so that the head of flat-head screws will pull down flush to the surface of the wood.

Caterwauling. Literally the sound of a cat in heat, used to describe the sound of machinery (especially a saw blade) that's spinning with a wobble and the resulting erratic cut.

Caulk. Any of a number of compounds that stay pliable over time and used to seal seams between materials on exterior surfaces or around water.

Cross Member. Used in various contexts to denote the materials that span a horizontal distance between points.

Cove Molding. A common molding from which a quarter cylinder of wood has been removed for decorative purposes.

Crown. The decorative work at the top of a construction as on a post or over a door and usually the most elaborately decorated portion of the component.

Dado. A groove in a board cut away to accept another board. Also the section of the wall in a Victorian house between the floor and the chair rail which was often covered by embossed wallpaper to add the appearance of heft to the wall.

Dormer. A window set upright projecting out of a slanted roof, with its own roof over it.

Double-Hung Window. A type of window with counter-balanced weights to hold it in an open position, built with an upper and lower pane of glass framed by wood.

Double Plumbing. A system of plumbing that runs pipe from the water main and the hot water heater directly to the bathroom so that other uses of water will not cause a pressure drop or temperature change in the shower.

Drill Press. A stand with a movable unit containing the drill so that holes can be drilled with precision by pulling down on a lever.

Dutch Door. A door cut in two horizontally in the middle so that the upper half can be opened without opening the lower half.

Fanciwork. Any of a wide variety of decorative work mass-produced by automatic woodworking machines and used to decorate Victorian houses.

Fascia Strip. (or fascia). A strip of wood used decoratively to separate components on the exterior of a house.

Filon. A fiberglass sheet available in rolls and commonly used to make low-cost translucent skylights.

Firestops. Short lengths of 2×4 (usually) nailed horizontally between studs to keep fire from spreading inside the wall.

Five-Quarter. Lumber thickness is expressed in quarters of an inch (1½-inch stock is called "six-quarter," 2-inch stock is called "eight-quarter" or "two-by"). Five-quarter is the rough measurement; dressed on both sides to a smooth finish the board will measure 1-1/16 inches. Five-quarter is commonly used for windowsills and stairtreads.

Flashing. Copper or galvanized steel strips used to control water runoff around windows, doors, dormers, chimneys or other interruptions of a roof or exterior wall.

Furring Strips. Thin strips of wood nailed to the studs to raise depressions or provide a nailing surface for the finish wall material.

Glazing Pins. Triangular pieces of steel used to hold glass in place before it is glazed (sealed with a material similar to caulk).

Gesso. A plaster of Paris compound used for molded ornaments on houses and furniture.

Green Lumber. Lumber which has not been dried either by exposure to air or through heat processing in a kiln. Less expensive than dried lumber, it is subject to warping if it dries unevenly.

Half-Round. A decorative molding in the shape of a half cylinder.

Header. The heavy horizontal framing member which spans the top of a window or door.

Heartwood. Lumber cut from the center of a log that was once the growing tip of the tree and is characterized by many small knots.

Joist. A heavy wood cross member which rests on beams and supports the floor or decking, or holds the ceiling.

Kitchen Queen. Brand name for a free standing cabinet unit containing a lower section of shelves or drawers, a counter and a raised section containing a cupboard with doors.

Lath. Thin strips of wood nailed to the studs of a wall to provide a base for plaster to make a lath-and-plaster wall.

Lead Caming. The lead strips that separate and hold glass in decorative windows.

Lineal Feet. A measurement of sawn lumber which takes into account only its length, as opposed to board feet, which accounts for the total amount of wood.

M. Shorthand for 1,000. Lumber in wholesale quantities is quoted as so many dollars per thousand board feet ($445M).

Massing. The relationship of horizontal and vertical volume combined in architecture to create an aesthetic effect.

Mastic. A thick paste adhesive with a variety of bases available in tubes, cans or cartridges.

Medallions. Plaster or gesso castings commonly glued to the ceiling of Victorian houses to emphasize and decorate hanging light fixtures.

Millings. Wood that has been milled or altered by being passed over various shaped blades.

Mud. Colloquial term for any material having the consistency of mud (e.g. taping compound, wet concrete) to be used on walls and in construction.

Nominal. The size of a board as it comes from the sawmill before planing smooths the surfaces. A 2×4 (nominal measurement) is planed to 1½ by 3½ actual inches.

One-By. The most commonly used trim thickness: 1 inch thick nominal; ¾ inch actual. One-by is available in a variety of widths: 1×1; 1×4; 1×6; 1×8; and so forth.

Open Face. A cut of lumber in which the grain of the wood is shown flat, forming long cathedral-shaped ellipses of grain. Open-face lumber is liable to curl as it continues to dry.

Particle Board. A composition board made of chips of wood mixed with glue and pressed into a sheet. Particle board is less expensive than plywood but lacks plywood's shear strength. Often used as a subfloor or in cabinet construction.

Parting Bead. The strip of wood which separates double-hung windows and forms a part of their tracks.

Penny. A measurement of nails formerly used to express their cost per hundred but now used to denote their strength. Abbreviated "−d." Higher numbers indicate larger nails.

Perf Tape. Perforated paper tape which adds fiber and tensile strength to seams in a plasterboard wall. The perforations allow the plaster on both sides of the tape to join.

Picture Hanging Strip. A strip of molding high on the wall of a Victorian house. Pictures are hung from the strip, avoiding the need to pound nails in the plaster.

Pin Knots. Knots in wood small enough to stay in place after the wood has dried and shrunk. Size varies with the species of wood.

Pitch. The slope of a roof, expressed as a ratio: "3:12" indicates a drop of 3 inches over a 12-inch distance.

Plinth. The base of a column that spreads the weight over the foundation. By extension, the larger base at the bottom of a door frame in some styles of ornamentation.

Pot-Belly Molding. A molding machined with a large half round at the bottom and a decorated top. Especially useful atop the kickplate where the smaller edge can be nailed tight and the pot belly will help hide irregularities in the wall.

Quarter Round. Molding in the shape of a quarter circle, commonly used where the floor meets the wall.

Quoin. Stone insets which protect the corners of brick buildings, sometimes duplicated on wood sided buildings as a decorative effect.

Rafter. A beam—usually 2×4—which runs from the ridge to the gutters and supports the roof.

Ripping. Sawing wood in the direction of the grain.

Riser. The vertical face plate that fills the space between the steps in a stairway.

Roof Safe. Assembly of copper or galvanized steel that surrounds projecting pipes and chimneys, that pierce a roof. A roof safe provides protection against leaking.

Rosette. See *Medallion*.

Router. A hand-held power tool used to shape the edge of boards in a decorative manner.

Sash. The wooden frame around the glass in a window.

Sash Weight. The weight hung in

the wall by cord to counter balance the weight of the window and sash.

Self-Rimming Sink. Most modern sinks are self-rimming, which means that the lip of the sink sits directly on the countertop with no need for a decorative trim strip to hide the joint. Caulk under the lip of the sink provides water tightness.

Shim. The use of a wedged piece of wood to make fine adjustments between two objects, usually a doorframe and the studs to which it is nailed. Two shims should oppose each other so that the final nailing surface does not have the slope of the wedge.

Shiplap. Boards milled to overlap one another so that rain will run down their outside surface. The most common type of wood siding for houses.

Sill. The horizontal plane which forms the bottom of the frame of a door or window.

Skim Coat. A very thin coat of plaster applied to fill cracks, nicks or other unevenness in a wall.

Sticker. Wood-milling machine used in the production of moldings and other lightly milled stock. Dry rough lumber runs on rollers through the sticker while shaper blades mill the four sides to a plain or decorative effect.

Stile. The vertical wooden frame component of a door or window.

Stringer. A heavy horizontal timber which spans the distance between posts and provides support for the joists that in turn support the flooring.

Stud. The upright 2×4s that form the basis of a wall. Commonly, any 2×4.

S4S—Tongue and Groove. A method of joining lumber along its long sides with one edge milled so that it has a projecting "tongue" which fits inside the groove milled in the neighboring piece. Often used for flooring.

Take Down. Colloquial for removing material in small increments.

Throw Bolt. A common type of door lock. The bolt rests in a holder fastened to the door; when it is slid into a latch on the door frame, the door cannot be opened.

Throw. Colloquial for the span between points.

Toenailing. A method of nailing used when direct access is restricted and the nail cannot be driven straight from one board to another. A toenail is driven at 45 degrees. Old fir should be drilled before toenailing is attempted.

Turnings. Wood which has been milled on a lathe by turning against a cutting blade. In modern lathe work, the wood stock revolves only once while the blades spin rapidly.

Twelve Gauge. The weight of copper wire used in room wiring for 110 volt sockets and lights.

Veneer. Thin cut wood used to make plywood or to put a quality facing on cheaper lumber in furniture. Common grades of veneer are peeled from the log and produce large characteristic open-faced grain. Fancy veneer for finish work is sawn rather than peeled to produce vertical grain.

Vertical Grain. Abbreviated VG. Lumber sawn across the annular rings to produce straight grain that will not curl.

Wainscotting. A wood dressing for walls that commonly reaches from the floor to a height of four or five feet.

Wall Sizing. A preparation similar to glue that seals a wall prior to painting or wallpapering.

Woodbutcher. A contemporary style of carpentry which emphasizes imagination and novelty in the use of materials at the expense of refinement of execution.

Wow. Colloquial for the curvature or warpage over the length of a board.

INDEX